Voices *of the* Night

WINNER, NAUTILUS BOOK AWARD

Better Books for a Better World

The Nautilus Awards seeks, honors, and promotes well-written and produced books that inspire and connect our lives and stimulate the imagination, offering the reader new possibilities for "a better life and a better world."

Past award winners include Deepak Chopra, Desmond Tutu, Jeremy Rifkin, Eckhart Tolle, and his holiness the Dalai Lama.

"It is our pleasure to welcome you to the honored and respected group of Nautilus Book Award Winners. You have written and published a book that carries a powerful message, and we are grateful for the opportunity to help promote and celebrate your book by making it visible as a Nautilus Book Award Winner."

—*Mary Belknap, Director, Nautilus Book Awards*

Voices of the Night

By
Gemma Cannon

Portland, Maine

Voices of the Night
P.O. Box 7832
Portland, ME 04112-7832

www.gemmacannon.com

Cover and Book Design by Grace Peirce

Voices of the Night is a work of inspirational non-fiction that includes the author's present recollection of past experiences over a period of years. The dialogue and events have been compressed to convey the substance of what was said or occurred, and the names of hospital patients have been changed to protect confidentiality.

ISBN 978-0-9913691-9-5

Library of Congress Control Number: 2013923726

Printed in the United States of America

Publisher's Cataloging-in-Publication Data

Cannon, Gemma.

Voices of the night / Gemma Cannon.

pages cm

Includes bibliographical references.

ISBN: 978-0-9913691-9-5 (pbk.)

ISBN: 978-0-9913691-8-8 (e-book)

1. Loss (Psychology) 2. Attitude to Death—Popular Works. 3. Spirituality. 4. Cancer—Patients. 5. Longfellow, Henry Wadsworth, 1807-1882. I. Title.

BF575.G7 C345 2014

155.9`3—dc23

2013923726

For my brother John and his children,
John and Alice, and for Dad, Billy, and
Sue of blessed memory.

Cambridge April 5, 1873

From a letter to a friend:

I am deeply touched and grieved by the melancholy tidings you send me. These are the sorrows to which all others are as nothing. They change us. We can never be again what we were before, though we may seem so to the eyes of others. But we know that a part of ourselves is gone, and cannot come back again.

I will not attempt to console you,—that is useless; but I suffer with you and share your affliction.

Yours affectionately,

Henry W. Longfellow

Contents

— Part One —

GRIEF

"They who go feel not the pain of parting; it is they who stay behind that suffer."

(from "Michael Angelo" by Henry Wadsworth Longfellow)

1

A Grief Story

ALL GRIEF STORIES ARE LOVE STORIES. WE ONLY grieve what we've loved and lost.

My grief story began with a phone call.

"It's Sue," my mother blurted, referring to my brother's wife and speaking in a rush of words. "There are spots on her liver. It may be from breast cancer or melanoma. Is that bad?"

My throat tightened as I heard the anxious, thin note in her voice. "It's serious, Mom," I said.

I tried to sound calm, but I'd worked for years as an oncology social worker. I knew too much about metastasized cancer to enjoy the luxury of denial.

"Maybe it isn't cancer," my mother continued. "Maybe it's an infection. There's no biopsy yet."

But when the biopsy results came in the following day, it wasn't an infection. It was a malignant tumor.

"The doctor gives her three to six months," my brother told my parents in a broken voice.

Three to six months! With the passing of each day, I dreaded the looming deadline.

I quickly planned a trip to England to visit Sue, my brother John, and their two small children in their London home.

We had five days together. We watched movies; we stayed up late; we ate lots of chocolate. We pretended we had a future and planned a trip to Italy. We celebrated life, but our denial of her illness couldn't last.

The day before my return to the States, Sue had an outpatient appointment with the radiologist. She asked me to come with her.

The taxi picked us up.

From the backseat of the hired car, I could see her four-year old son at the front-parlor window. He pressed his little hands hard against the glass and watched us, his eyes wide above his frowning mouth. When the taxi pulled away, he began to wave.

Sue fluttered her hands in return. Putting on the bravest front, she gave him her largest smile. She turned to me in the back seat. "Isn't he sweet?" she said.

We arrived at London's Royal Marsden Hospital. The open windows let in the August breeze and provided relief from the heavy air.

Sue led me to a small waiting room. We poured ourselves a cup of coffee and sat on the edge of a sofa, opposite a family from Saudi Arabia. With the solemnity of people who congregate in a cancer center, we nodded at each other over paper cups until a voice called out Sue's name.

We met privately with the nurse.

"It may not be anything," Sue began, "but I can't lift my arm." To demonstrate her lack of mobility, she tried to raise it. "It hurts too much," she said.

"Maybe this is how it's going to be," the nurse gently replied.

The calm timbre of her voice alarmed me. I recognized the measured cadence from my work on the oncology unit. It was the deliberate tone used by doctors, nurses, and social workers when patients were too sick to get better.

I then knew Sue would never lift her arm. She would never be pain-free without drugs. These would be my last hours with her.

As if she understood the nurse's unspoken words, Sue had nothing more to say. The nurse scheduled an appointment with the doctor for the following week, and we left the hospital by bus.

Most likely, Sue wanted to run away and hide. Instead, she moved onward with a quest. She'd promised me bed linens from Harrods as a wedding gift, and not even cancer would get in her way.

I could barely keep up as she barreled through the world's largest department store.

"When Princess Diana shops here," she told me, "they lock the doors." Like a guide on a historic house tour, Sue gave running commentary as we ascended the floors. "You can get anything at Harrods. Goldie Hawn bought an elephant here." We whizzed through Bridal. "My mother bought her wedding dress here," she told me, "the last sold during World War II."

Her shopping skills were predator-sharp, and we moved swiftly to the bed linen department. I found the perfect regal-red duvet in a classic British print.

Sue scoffed at the sale price. "How embarrassing!" she pronounced. "You must buy more!"

I resisted, but she insisted, adding bed sheets and pillow shams to the wedding gift mix. Generosity had always been part of her nature.

Mission accomplished, we adjourned to a tearoom for tea and scones. But without the rush of shopping to distract us, a pall fell over our table as we waited for our server.

Oh! How I wanted to make it better—to make it all go away—but I couldn't. I wanted to hold her hand and say the right words, but I couldn't do that either. Trying not to cry, I blinked back my tears.

I felt both the fullness of my love and the fullness of my grief. "I just want you to know," I finally blurted through the ache at the back of my throat, "how we all love you. You have been the most marvelous thing ever to happen to John."

"Why?" she queried. "What do you mean?"

Her question staggered me. "You don't *know*?" I asked in return. "How could you not know?"

Before meeting Sue, my brother—an international corporate attorney—had been consumed by work. For a long time, unrelieved stress had compromised his health. But after meeting Sue, he'd found balance again. His health had returned, and he had become happy, even playful. A blessed marriage followed a storybook wedding, and a son and daughter doubled their joy. My brother had never been more content.

How could she not know?

Amid the tea-time chatter surrounding us, I tried to make clear to her what had been obvious to me. I told her she'd transformed his life. She was my brother's evening star that illumined the night sky. With her, he'd found his way.

As Sue listened, the features on her face constricted.

Perhaps my words shocked her. Maybe she now knew that I, who knew a lot about cancer through my work, had started to believe she was dying.

Dear Sue! To me, she was more than a sister-in-law; she was a sister-in-heart. Although separated by an ocean, we dressed in the same style, wore the same perfume, read the same books, enjoyed the same movies, and drank the same blend of loose tea.

I couldn't imagine life without her.

I wanted to tell her how much I loved her and how much my family loved her. I wanted to tell her she was the perfect partner for my brother, a wonderful sister to me, and a marvelous mother to her children. I had much to say but couldn't speak. My eyes felt too swollen and my throat too tight.

Our food came. The waiter placed a bowl of clotted cream in the middle of the table.

"You can't get clotted cream in America." I tried to sound casual as I applied a dollop to my scone.

"Oh, I wish I'd known sooner," Sue responded with a twinge of regret. "We could have gotten some for you at Harrods."

Her silver spoon circled the rim of her china cup as inner concerns stole her attention. In her haunted expression, I could see the realization of her impending death.

There was nothing for either of us to say. No words could contain the meaning of the moment. No words could mitigate the pain.

An inner ache replaced all appetite, and without finishing our pastries, we left the tearoom for our sad ride home.

When the bus arrived, Sue pulled herself up the narrow stairs and climbed to the top of the double-decker. Then she took my hand, and drawing me beside her, she slid into the best seat on London's transit: on top and up front.

I'll always remember this about her. She still had choices. She could have collapsed into the easiest, closest seat. Instead, she reached for the stairs to watch the world go by from the upper deck.

Six weeks later, Sue died.

With her passing, the world became a cold, dark place. With her passing, images seemed to blur and colors to fade. With her passing, a great light went out, and consolation was nowhere to be found.

2

How Do We Live with Grief When It Won't Go Away?

HOW LONG DOES GRIEF LAST?

In the early eighties, when I was a student at Columbia University's School of Social Work, the conventional wisdom was "one year." After one year of exposure to birthdays, holidays, and anniversaries, the experts decreed the bereaved should "be over it," or something "is wrong." In the late eighties, the experts extended the duration of grief to two years. Soon afterward, it became three years. Then it became five years.

What is the right answer? Eager to know, I turned to my mother who held sad knowledge about grief.

Years earlier, her four-month-old daughter had died a crib death. My mother often told me how, during the weeks following the death of her baby, she'd sit before her easel with a paintbrush in her hand. For hours, she'd work in a trance-like state as she coated the canvas with broad strokes of color.

Years later, she remarked on her surprise when, while sweeping hair from her eyes during a brief break, her fingers had grazed against cheeks covered with tears. Until that moment, she told me, she hadn't realized she'd been silently weeping as she worked.

But that was long ago. Since then, she'd raised five children. She'd been a master-teacher in the Connecticut school system. And through it all, she'd smiled often and laughed a lot.

To me, she hadn't seemed sad at all.

So when I asked my mother, "How long does it take to get over it," I expected her to give me a number: one year, three years, or five years. Her answer surprised me.

"You never get over it," she said.

How could that be? I thought. According to the experts, my mother should be "over it" by now, but it didn't matter what the professionals said. For my mother, the acuity of her grief had ended but not the grief itself.

That's when I first perceived the invisibility and silence of grief. All these years, my mother had harbored a deep sorrow, and all these years, I'd been blind and deaf to it. I couldn't see or hear the sadness in her heart.

It left me with a lingering question: *If we don't "get over grief," how do we live with it?*

Faith sustains some of us, but what about the rest of us? Where can we turn when personal tragedy mocks our faith and taunts us with troubled thoughts? What do we do if grief—in a staggering, double loss—robs us of core beliefs when comfort is most needed?

"The real danger," writes C.S. Lewis following the death of his wife, "is not to stop believing in God; the real danger is coming to believe such dreadful things about him."

In other words, the danger is to see God as I saw God: a puppeteer manipulating his marionettes in a wicked pantomime. One lift of the strings, and we dance! One dip of the strings, and we fall!

Who can trust such a God? When we lose that trust, what can sustain us? Is there no relief, no refreshment for the spirit?

How can we find consolation?

As a young social worker, I'd been clinically trained to counsel cancer patients and their family members, but my skills and academic background couldn't answer the questions that hounded me.

"Try to live *the questions* themselves," advises the German poet Rainer Maria Rilke in a letter to a friend. "*Live* the questions now. Perhaps you will then gradually, without noticing it, live along some distant day into the answer."

I followed Rilke's guidance and lived the question, "How do we live with grief when it won't go away?"

The answer eluded me.

"Do not now seek the answers," Rilke advises, "which cannot be given you, because you would not be able to live them. And the point is, to live everything."

I followed Rilke's suggestion and stopped searching for answers, but the questions pursued me. For respite, I sequestered myself in the library and read nineteenth-century periodicals in a time-travel escape.

I wanted, as Rilke counseled, "to live everything." So I indulged my passion for the past and became a guide at the boyhood home of Henry Wadsworth Longfellow, America's celebrated nineteenth-century poet.

Here, when I wasn't looking, I found a teacher who answered my questions.

I had lived my way into the answers.

3

Living the Question

HENRY WADSWORTH LONGFELLOW DIED IN 1882.

More than a hundred years later, I prepared a tour of his boyhood home in Portland, Maine. As part of my research, I sat in the Portland Room of our public library and read through journal entries, letters, and biographies.

I soon learned he was no stranger to grief and loss.

Before turning thirty, Longfellow had buried both sets of grandparents, his oldest sister and his youngest sister, his best friend who was also his brother-in-law, and his own young bride. He married again, and within a few years, he buried his baby daughter. Then an alcoholic brother died, leaving three young children without parents to raise them. The deaths of his parents followed.

Perhaps most traumatic was the death of Fanny, his second wife, who burned to death when a stray match ignited her gown. On fire and screaming for help, she ran into Longfellow's study. Acting quickly, he wrapped her body in a blanket and used his hands to keep the flames from her face, but he couldn't save her. She died the next day.

Longfellow's fight for Fanny's life left him with severe burns on his hands and face, and after the fire, he never shaved again.

His signature beard became a daily reminder of the inferno that killed his wife and left him the single father of five children; the eldest was eighteen, and the youngest was seven.

But despite great grief, Longfellow didn't isolate or self-destruct. Instead, he consoled readers worldwide through his poetry. He was the most widely-read author of his time.

How did he do it? How did he brave multiple tragedies yet find the courage to live an engaged and productive life?

I needed to know.

To find answers, I parked myself in the Portland Room of our public library. Like a detective, I scoped out biographies and poured though his letters and journal entries.

I began with the dates following Fanny's death.

At the time of the fatal accident, Longfellow had already attained international fame. By today's standards, he held rock-star status on the world-wide cultural stage. But he was a reluctant celebrity who valued his privacy, and his letters and journal notes following the fire are self-consciously evasive. Although Fanny's death had left him a broken man, his writing conceals his anguish and provides no clues to his coping strategies.

So I hunted through earlier letters and journals, written before Longfellow's literary fame had compromised full disclosure of his thoughts and feelings.

While reading his youthful entries, I lingered over pages filled with raw emotion, desire, courtship, and hope. Between the lines, a lovely young woman—no more than a footnote in most Longfellow biographies—emerged from the shadows. She engaged me like a Jane Austen heroine and revealed an earlier story of love and loss that turned my attention to a younger Longfellow and his radiant first wife, Mary Potter.

* * *

For decades, Mary's family would tell the story of how the

young couple met and how they fell in love.

Longfellow, twenty-three years old, had just completed his first year as Professor of Modern Languages at Bowdoin College in Brunswick, Maine. It had been a grueling introduction to the teaching profession.

In 1829, the study of Modern Languages was a new discipline. Longfellow, as one of the subject's first teachers, didn't have the luxury of pre-published lessons and books. Without access to time-tested resources, he needed to produce his own, so he created both the curriculum for his students to follow and the college textbooks for them to use.

He published the books himself with a keen eye for detail. His careful supervision, from proof-sheet corrections to the selection of purple cloth for the binding, indicated that nothing was too good for his students.

His scholars may have been too young to appreciate his efforts. They were schoolboys, only fourteen years old when they left home for college, and prone to playing pranks. When their behavior became a growing concern, the Bowdoin College leadership pressed Longfellow, who was popular among the boys, to provide discipline.

In addition to teaching Spanish and French and publishing textbooks, he was now expected to regulate student behavior. It was a lot to ask of the young professor, and Longfellow felt burdened and unrewarded. "You call it a dog's life: it is indeed—my dear Anne," he later writes his sister. "I do not believe I was born for such a lot..."

No doubt, he looked forward to the end of term and a visit to his boyhood home in Portland, Maine.

It was an appealing destination. At the time, Portland was regionally famous for its beautiful women, and after a year of teaching Modern Languages to teen-aged boys, he would have likely welcomed the change of venue.

He wasn't happy, and his family noticed his discontent. His discerning brother observes that, although Longfellow expressed interest in his work and his students, "Something was still wanting."

It wouldn't be long before Longfellow could identify the source of his deficiency. While joining his family for the Sunday service at the First Parish Church, the young man could finally see what he lacked.

"Among the ladies," writes his brother, "whose beauty kept up the reputation of his native town, now conspicuous was the daughter of his father's friend and neighbor, Judge Barrett Potter."

The Judge's daughter sat with her father and her two lovely sisters in the Potter family pew.

Longfellow, from his own family pew, had good view of the dark haired beauty with deep blue eyes. He recognized the family and presumed that she was Mary, the judge's second daughter.

They'd attended grammar school together. Mary was only five years old when he'd last seen her; he was only ten. She'd grown since then, and he couldn't help but notice how much she'd changed.

When the service ended, he found himself following her down the aisle of the First Parish Church and out its doors.

Mary, while strolling home with her family, may not have been aware of the young man traipsing behind them. Even if she had noticed him, she would not have been able to acknowledge him. Nineteenth-century protocol required a formal introduction before a lady could engage a gentleman in conversation.

Propriety also prevented Longfellow from initiating an exchange. Bound by the same social constraints as Mary, he could only gaze at her from a respectful distance.

Frustrated, he quickly formed a plan.

His sister Anne, Mary's good friend, was well-positioned to orchestrate a proper introduction, so Longfellow hastened to his family home. "He begged his sister to call with him at once at the Potter residence," writes a family member, "and all the rest followed, as in a novel."

Mary proved a fitting partner for the college professor.

Unlike most girls of her time, she'd received an excellent education. While attending the celebrated Cushing School in Hingham, Massachusetts, she'd studied European history and literature, among other subjects.

Her schoolgirl notebooks had been kept by her family for years. Remarkable among the findings were a series of astronomy lectures, accurately recorded by the young Mary from memory.

According to Longfellow biographer Thomas Wentworth Higginson, it wasn't only astronomy notes that reveal her intellect. All her school papers, abstracts and compositions, he tells us, show a thoughtful and well-trained mind. "Some exhibit a metaphysical turn," he writes, "others are girlish studies in history and geography; but the love of literature is visible everywhere, in copious extracts from the favorite authors of that day, even Coleridge and Shelley."

The Potter family reports that Mary had never learned Latin or Greek, as her father disapproved of these studies for girls. Judge Potter, however, had "encouraged her in the love of mathematics," writes Higginson, "and there is, among her papers, the calculation of an eclipse."

Mary not only had a mind suitable to partner Longfellow in his work, but she also had good temperament. "She was a lovely woman in character and appearance," her next door neighbor recalls, "gentle, refined, and graceful, with an attractive manner that won all hearts."

Her graceful character, as well as her beauty and intellect, appealed to Longfellow. "I have never seen a woman," he writes her father, "in whom every look and word and action seemed to proceed from so gentle and innocent a spirit."

When Longfellow engaged her affection, he considered himself highly privileged.

They were married at the First Parish Unitarian Church on September 14, 1831. She was nineteen; he was twenty-four.

A professor at Bowdoin College described them both. "My first impression of her," he writes, "is of an attractive person, blooming in health and beauty, the graceful bride of a very attractive and elegant young man."

They set up housekeeping in a cottage near Bowdoin College, and every night the scent of pine burned in the air as they sat by their fireside. On some evenings, Longfellow would listen to the rhythmic scratch of Mary's quill pen as she copied quotations from the poets into his lectures. On other evenings, she would sew by the light of the fire while he played a soft melody on his flute.

"They were tenderly devoted to each other," Longfellow's brother writes, "and never was there a home more happy than theirs."

With Mary as his helpmate, Longfellow continued to distinguish himself as a foreign language scholar and teacher. His reputation flourished, and he was soon offered the prestigious post as Smith Professor of Modern Languages and Belle Lettres at Harvard University.

He accepted the professorship, but there was one caveat. Harvard required a command of the German language that he hadn't yet mastered, and Longfellow believed he'd need further study to meet the obligations of his new appointment. So the young couple departed for Europe, to expand Longfellow's knowledge of German in preparation for his new position.

Clara Crowninshield, a friend of Mary's, joined them. They'd attended school together, and Clara would be a fine companion for Mary during Longfellow's extended hours of study.

They began their trip on a high note and traveled to London, Sweden, and Finland. Throughout the journey, Mary sent travel narratives to their families in Portland, and in her correspondence, she included letters to Longfellow's mother and aunt.

She seems to have enjoyed herself. "We are generally taken for French," she writes her mother-in-law, "and I am always believed to be Henry's sister. They say to me, 'What a resemblance between your brother and self!'"

Mary was among the first generation of daughters born into America's newly-minted Republic, so it's not surprising that, when describing the English aristocracy, she finds little value in their self-importance. She reserves her praise for their literary friends, Thomas and Jane Carlyle. "Mr. and Mrs. Carlyle have more genuine worth and talent than half of the nobility in London," she writes her mother-in-law. "Mr. Carlyle's literary fame is very high, and she is a very talented woman—but they are people after my own heart—not the least pretension about them."

In her letter-writing, she was sensitive to her husband's retiring aunt who had helped to raise him. "My dear Aunt Lucia," she writes, "Pray do not be alarmed on receiving this letter for fear that you must answer it. I have not hoped such a favor, but am content, however much I should be delighted to hear from you, to write you occasionally without the hopes of an answer, and thinking and knowing you would be as happy to receive a letter from me as any of my dear friends."

Mary also writes Longfellow's father. After learning of his feeble health, she sent him pages of carefully copied entries from her husband's journal. "If it cheers a lonely winter's evening," she writes him, "or cheats you of a few melancholy hours, I shall feel most amply repaid for the trouble I have taken."

The Potter and Longfellow families would have anticipated the happy dispatches written in Mary's hand, and it's easy to imagine them reading the letters aloud by the fireside in the parlor. No doubt, they would have also noted that her letters stopped when Henry and Mary reached Amsterdam.

Unbeknownst to their loved ones in Maine, Mary had suffered a miscarriage.

It wasn't her first terminated pregnancy. She'd been through a previous miscarriage in Brunswick, but now she lay bleeding in a darkened hotel chamber far from home.

In the blackness of night, Longfellow rummaged through their trunks for flannel to absorb the blood flowing from Mary's body. But their last candle had burned to a stub, and he could hardly see. Panicked, he knocked on Clara's door.

Longfellow didn't tell her why he needed emergency light and cloth, as it would have been indelicate for a man to mention pregnancy or miscarriage to a lady. Clara could only guess the source of his distress as she scavenged through her travel chest for wax tapers and fabric. As she handed him her supply, she feared for her friend.

Three weeks later, Mary assured them she felt strong enough to resume their journey. Happy to leave Amsterdam, the Longfellow party hired a carriage and traveled to Rotterdam where they engaged rooms in a hotel.

The apartment was elegant. Stucco plastered the high ceilings, and a wool Brussels carpet covered the cold floor, but it was dark. "We are unfortunately on the north side of the house," writes Clara in her journal, "so that not a ray of sunshine visits us through the day."

For the next month, Mary got up each morning, shared breakfast with her husband in their bedchamber, and rested as he read aloud to her. She had good appetite and encouraged the others she felt better, but with pain throbbing through her head and limbs, her health quickly declined.

A local physician came to examine her. Mary could see him frown as he assessed her condition, and she could hear him discuss her case with her husband in the hallway.

The look on the doctor's face and the tone in his voice confirmed what she already knew—she would never be well again. When Clara offered a dose of medicine, Mary refused it. "It won't do me any good, Clara," she said.

She hadn't felt well for months. After they'd left England, chills and fever had often kept Mary from joining the others on sight-seeing adventures. She'd been bed-bound and sick for so long, perhaps she'd feared her own death when sending a letter to her father only six weeks earlier:

> How often I recall you as I saw you the sad morning that we parted! It could not be otherwise than a very sad morning to us all, for we felt that it was very possible we were saying our last goodbye to some dear one…

According to Mary's niece, these words were later underlined in pencil by Judge Potter, to whom they were written, and the paper folded and unfolded several times. The bereaved father could not have known, when first reading it, that his daughter lay dying in a dark hotel room far from home.

Clara and Longfellow kept vigil by her side. Clara took the day shift while Longfellow sat by her bed through the night.

One evening, in a fit of fever, Mary's bed cap slipped from her head. Longfellow couldn't help but notice how pale her face looked against the darkness of her hair. When he leaned over to kiss her lips, and she didn't kiss him back, he stumbled out of the room.

"My poor Mary is worse today," he writes in his journal. "Sinking—sinking. My poor heart is heavy, yet I hope, perhaps too fondly."

Four days later, Mary felt a slight oppression in her chest and could hardly breathe. Longfellow, to ease the pressure, piled pillows beneath her until she almost sat upright in bed. "Are you breathing easier?" he asked.

"Yes, dear," she answered.

But despite his efforts, her breathing remained shallow and labored. He couldn't hide his alarm at her condition.

In death as in life, Longfellow later writes her cousin, Mary was more mindful of others than of herself. His anxiety didn't escape her attention, and true to character, she attempted to relieve his distress.

"Why should I be troubled?" she reassured him, even as she struggled to breathe. "If I should die, God will take me to himself."

From that moment on, Longfellow writes Judge Potter, Mary was perfectly calm, except for a single instant when she remembered her adored, widowed father.

"O, my dear Father!" she cried out, sensitive to his eminent grief. "How he will mourn for me."

She then spent her remaining minutes to express her love and care for others. She began with Clara.

Through weeks of ill health, Clara had nursed her, and Mary—sensitive to her friend's sadness—addressed her with these last, tender words. "Dear, good little Clara," she managed to say as Clara placed compresses of brandy-soaked flannel on her chest.

Nor did she forget her many friends back home who would grieve her death. "Tell all my friends," she urged her husband, "I thought of them at the last hour."

Clara notes that, as Mary lay dying, she spoke with the most perfect composure and seemed conscious she was near her end.

"My father has always been kind to me, and so have all

my friends," she stated without distress.

"Because you have always been a good, gentle girl," Longfellow responded.

"Will God take me to him?"

"Yes."

"I shall see my dear mother, shan't I?"

Clara watched as Mary clasped Longfellow's neck with her almost lifeless arm.

"Henry, it is hard to die and leave you. I remember all your kindness to me."

He consoled her through remembrance of Mary's beloved mother who had died when she was nine. "You are going to your own best friend," he said.

"Dear Henry," she whispered, "do not forget me!"

They held each other in one final embrace. "I will be with you and watch over you," she promised with her last words and kissed him before letting go.

She died a few hours later, Longfellow by her side.

Mary's loyal friend, who had become like a sister to both of them, witnessed his sorrow from an adjoining room. "Now that there was no longer cause for restraint," writes Clara, "he gave vent to his grief and wept bitterly till sleep came to his relief."

The next day, Longfellow completed the sad tasks of the newly bereaved. He made arrangements for burial and scheduled passage on a packet ship to carry Mary's body across the ocean. He jotted her name and age on a piece of paper and placed it in her coffin. He pulled the rings from her fingers and placed them on his own.

But perhaps what pained him most was to kiss her cold lips and to write Mary's father a detailed account of her death. He ends his letter to Judge Potter with this quote from Shelley, one of Mary's favorite poets:

> Peace! Peace! She is not dead, she does not sleep! She has wakened from the dream of life!

These words may have given him the needed strength to pack his bags, buy tickets, and reserve lodging in Heidelberg, despite the last words written in Mary's journal: "If I get to Heidelberg, I should be so happy."

A period of initial numbness allowed him to make plans for weeks of study and travel, but grief soon knocked him to his knees with full force.

"I feel lonely and dejected," he writes his father, "and the recollection of the last three months of my life overwhelms me with unceasing sorrow."

It's typical for the bereaved, even in the deep rawness of early grief, to find pauses between waves of pain. For Longfellow, these grief gaps allowed him to play cards, walk through town, and study the German authors, but respite was brief. When some familiar voice, face, or object reminded him of Mary, a wave of sorrow would return and shatter him to the core of his soul.

"When I think how gentle and affectionate and good she was," he writes, "every moment of her life, even to the last, and she will be no more with me in the world and the sense of my bereavement is deep and unutterable."

Longfellow tried to write in his journal, but for the first time in his life, prose failed him. Instead, night after night, he copied the sonnet John Milton had composed to honor his own deceased wife, his "late espoused saint" who had died in childbirth.

In his poem, Milton sees her in his dream:

> But, oh! As to embrace me she inclined, I waked, she fled,
> and day brought back my night.

After inscribing Milton's sad sonnet into his journal, Longfellow filled the pages with four simple words of his own:

"To Mary in heaven, to Mary in heaven."

He grieved privately. By his own admission, he feigned a cheerful affect by day and wept only at night when he was alone. Acquaintances could not have guessed the depths of his suffering, but he's more forthright in his correspondence. "I take no part in what is going on around me," he writes in a letter to a friend.

The brooding young man turned to his books where he found a soul-companion in Novalis, the German poet who'd written the mystical "Hymns to the Night" after the death of his betrothed. In his poetry, Novalis reflects how, while weeping over the grave of his beloved, he'd felt her presence in the solitude of night.

Longfellow sensed a similar connection with Mary. "I feel assured of her presence," he writes in his journal. "O my beloved Mary—teach me to be good, and kind, and gentle as thou wert when here on earth…"

But grief made concentration difficult, and his command of German suffered for it. "I cannot study," he writes his mentor. "One thought occupies me night and day. She is dead—she is dead! All day I am weary and sad—and at night I cry myself to sleep like a child. Not a page can I read without my thoughts wandering from it."

To make it worse, he was far from friends and far from home, which only intensified his sorrow. "I am completely crushed to the earth," he writes his confidante, "and I have no friend with me to cheer me and console me."

Job commitments added to his burden, and he strained to complete his work. To honor his agreement with Harvard, Longfellow forced himself to study the German language and its authors.

He found himself drawn to Goethe, the German author of *Faust* and *Werther*, who offered a new life vision: to live a life worthy of a beautiful soul. The concept appealed to

Longfellow, but he was unable to answer Goethe's call to action. Bereavement had sapped him of the vitality he'd need to change his world view.

Too burdened by grief to be bold, and with energy only to travel and study, he left for Salzburg.

Sorrow pursued him.

While resting by a lake, church bells so vividly recalled the chimes he'd heard when Mary had died that a wave of grief pounded him with brute force.

Longfellow staggered up the hill toward the ringing bells. As he approached the churchyard, he could see a young girl leading a funeral procession. She held in her arms the body of an infant wrapped in a sheet.

He watched as she stopped at a hollow of freshly broken earth and rested her little bundle into the ground. Peasants, young and old, followed her with burning tapers in their hands. Each of them threw a handful of dirt over the baby's body before continuing into the church for the requiem mass.

Longfellow waited for the funeral procession to pass before he entered the churchyard. It was now empty, save for the digger of the baby's grave. The infant had been born in the night, the gravedigger told him, and had lived for one hour only.

The mourners had filled the church, but no one occupied the small chapel on the property. The stone structure seemed to welcome him with its open door, so he stumbled through the portal, and dropping to his knees, he wept.

He needed no infant's funeral to remind him of the death of his wife and their unborn child. He needed no lesson on the brevity of life, or that "from dust we are and to dust returneth."

After a while, he raised his eyes, and through his tears, looked on the tablet mounted on the chapel wall facing him. As he read the engraving, he learned that he'd been kneeling at the grave of a young nobleman who'd died twenty-five years earlier.

He describes his experience in his semi-autobiographical novel *Hyperion:*

> And now the sun was growing high and warm. A little chapel, whose door stood open, seemed to invite him to enter and enjoy the grateful coolness. He went in. There was no one there. The walls were covered with paintings and sculpture of the rudest kind, and with a few funeral tablets. There was nothing there to move the heart to devotion; but in that hour his heart was weak,—weak as a child's. He bowed his stubborn knees, and wept. And, how many disappointed hopes, how many bitter recollections, how much of wounded pride and requited love, were in those tears through which he read, on a marble tablet in the chapel wall opposite, this singular inscription:
>
> "Look not mournfully into the Past. It comes not back again. Wisely improve the Present. It is thine. Go forth to meet the shadowy Future, without fear, and with a manly heart."
>
> It seemed to him as if the unknown tenant of that grave had opened his lips of dust, and spoken to him the words of consolation, which his soul needed, and which no friend had yet spoken. In a moment the anguish of his thoughts was still. The stone was rolled away from the door of his heart; death was no longer there, but an angel clothed in white. He stood up, and his eyes were no more bleared with tears; and, looking into the bright morning heaven, he said:
>
> "I will be strong!"

The words of consolation transformed him.

Ambition had long consumed him. As a boy, he had dreamed of becoming a writer. When he graduated from Bowdoin College in 1825, the eighteen-year-old Longfellow had urged his classmates, including Nathaniel Hawthorne, to help create an American literature as the country was young, and few

American works had yet been published. He'd wanted American writers to emulate European authors and provide the public with stories to capture the nation's narrative. To contribute to the cause, he'd aimed for his own literary fame so as to lift his country's standing on the worldwide stage.

Ambition had made him restless to succeed, but his experience in the graveyard changed his priorities. After watching the burial of a baby, kneeling at the grave of the young nobleman, and reading the inscription on the chapel wall, he'd gained new appreciation for the life principles that Goethe had taught him.

Influenced by Goethe, the young man buried in the churchyard grave, and the infant who had lived a full life in an hour, Longfellow made a new vow. From that moment forward, he promised to "live in the Present wisely," "to become a man of action and reality," and "to live in his sphere and not wish it otherwise." He also decided to abandon corrosive ambition and the restlessness that forbade contentment.

"Live in the Present," he later writes a friend as he shared his post-tomb insights. "I find no other way of keeping my nerves quiet than this—namely, to do with all my might whatever I have to do, without thinking of the future, in which most people live."

For the bereaved, pre-occupation with the past and fantasies about the future can feel more psychologically safe than a focus on the present with all its sorrow and heartbreak. Despite his sadness, Longfellow resisted the impulse to escape. Instead, he chose to improve the present and courageously face his future.

In his conscious decision to deliberately live his life, he developed a reality-based action plan that included acceptance of his situation, a philosophy found in today's Serenity Prayer:

> God grant me the serenity to accept the things I cannot change, the courage to change the things I can, and the wisdom to know the difference.

But neither a new life view nor busy activity could dissolve his anguish or alleviate his grief.

"Travel is not always a cure for sadness," he writes. "So far from dissipating my thoughts, it concentrated them so that in this experiment of moral alchemy—this search after the sorcerer's stone—this turning of lead into gold—the crucible was near burst asunder."

"Oh, what a solitary lonely being I am!" he cries. "Why do I travel? Every hour, my heart aches."

Like many who grieve, Longfellow battered himself with guilt. When he counseled a friend to be good to his wife, he spoke from personal experience. "Never let one thought, word, or deed of yours be such as to throw a shadow upon her gentle spirit, as you value your own peace of mind hereafter," he warned. "These things give sharpness to the shafts of death; and these are the words of one 'who has himself been hurt by the archer.'"

Despite bouts with guilt and sorrow, he remained determined to follow the graveyard message—to live in the present—and decided to spend time in Switzerland with the Appleton family of Boston.

In the presence of young Fanny, whom he would later marry, he felt life stir within him for the first time since Mary had died. Fanny helped him translate poetry, and she showed him sketches in her notebook. In these lovely idylls of everyday life, Fanny helped him hope again.

Still, sorrow would not cease. Grief is great, and not even future promise could mitigate his sadness. A couple of weeks after his visit with the Appleton family, he attended a festival outside Paris that exposed his heartache. He writes in his journal:

> The day was pleasant, without shifting clouds and sunshine. They told me I was in good spirits. It was the surface only, stirred by the passing breeze and catching the sunshine of

> the moment. I have often observed, amid a chorus of a hundred voices and the sound of a hundred instruments—amid all the whirlwind of the vexed air—that I could distinguish the melancholy vibration of a single string, touched by a finger. It had a mournful, sobbing sound. Thus, amid the splendour of a festival—the rushing crowd, and song and sounds of gladness and a thousand mingling emotions—distinctly audible to the mind's ear are the pulsations of some melancholy chord of the heart touched by the finger of memory. And it has a mournful, throbbing sound.

He returned to America to begin his new position at Harvard University. From the solitude of his study, he writes Mary's sister of the "wound that will never entirely heal."

> Cambridge, Sunday evening (1836)
>
> My Dear Eliza,—
>
> By tomorrow's steamboat I shall send you two trunks, containing the clothes which once belonged to your sister. What I suffered in getting them ready to send to you, I cannot describe. It is not necessary, that I should.
>
> Cheerful as I may have seemed to you at times, there are other times, when it seems to me that my heart would break. The world considers grief unmanly, and is suspicious of that sorrow, which is expressed by words and outward signs. Hence we strive to be gay and put a cheerful courage on, when our souls are very sad. But there are hours, when the world is shut out, and we can no longer hear the voices, that cheer and encourage us. To me such hours come daily.
>
> I was so happy with my dear Mary that it is very hard to be alone. The sympathies of friendship are doubtless something—but after all how little, how unsatisfying they are to one who has been so loved as I have been.
>
> This is a selfish sorrow, I know; but neither reason nor reflection can still it. Affliction makes us childish. A

grieved and wounded heart is hard to be persuaded. We do not wish to have our sorrow lessened. There are wounds, which are never entirely healed.

A thousand associations call up the past, with all its gloom and shadow. Often a mere look or sound—a voice—the odor of a flower—the most trifle is enough to awaken within me deep and unutterable emotions. Hardly a day passes, that some face, or familiar object, or some passage in the book I am reading does not call up the image of my beloved wife so vividly, that I pause and burst into tears—and sometimes cannot rally again for hours.

And yet, my dear Eliza, in a few days, and we shall all be gone, and others sorrowing and rejoicing as we now do, will have taken our places; and we shall say, how childish it was for us to mourn for things so transitory. There may be some consolation in this; but we are nevertheless children. Our feelings overcome us.

Farewell. Give my kind regards to all, and believe me most truly and affectionately,

Your friend,
Henry W. Longfellow

He is twenty-nine years old when he writes this letter. With one exception, Longfellow hadn't written a poem since his youth, but that changed following his return from Europe. Inspired by Mary and the German mystic poet Novalis, he turns again to poetry.

For a year, he contemplates a poem about his beloved young wife. On his (uncelebrated) thirty-first birthday, he begins it:

When the hours of day are numbered,
And the voices of the night
Wake the better soul that slumbered
To a holy, calm delight;

He writes in a room lit by fire where candles throw shadows on the pattern-papered walls:

Ere the evening lamps are lighted
And, like phantoms grim and tall,
Shadows from the fitful firelight
Dance upon the parlor wall;

Under cover of night, his departed companions return:

Then the forms of the departed
Enter at the open door;
The beloved, the true-hearted,
Come to visit me once more;

Among them, he meets attorney George Pierce, his vibrant friend and brother-in-law, who'd died only days before Mary, struck down by typhus:

He, the young and strong who cherished
Noble longings for the strife,
By the roadside fell and perished,
Weary with the march of Life!

He remembers so many dear, dead loved ones: Eliza, his sister and confidante, with only a year between them, dead at twenty-one from tuberculosis; his youngest sister, Ellen, dead at seventeen from typhus; and his beloved grandparents, whose fireside stories had cultivated his active imagination:

They, the holy ones and weakly
Who the cross of suffering bore,
Folded their pale hands so meekly,
Spake with us on earth no more!

Then he sees Mary:

And with them the Being Beauteous,
Who unto my youth was given,
More than all things else to love me,
And is now a saint in heaven.

He eagerly anticipates her arrival:

With a slow and noiseless footstep
Comes that messenger divine,
Takes the vacant chair beside me,
Lays her gentle hand in mine.

He marvels at her:

And she sits and gazes at me
With those deep and tender eyes,
Like the stars, so still and saint-like,
Looking downward from the skies.

He receives her love:

Uttered not, yet comprehended,
Is the spirit's voiceless prayer,
Soft rebukes, in blessings ended,
Breathing from her lips of air.

Although sad and depressed, he experiences the truth of Mary's last words to him, "I will always be with you." Through connection to Mary and his beloved dead, he overcomes his fear:

Oh, though oft depressed and lonely,
All my fears are laid aside,
If I but remember only
Such as these have lived and died!

Longfellow labored over his manuscript. He typically completed his short poems in a few days or weeks, but it took him two years to complete this one. He writes in his journal:

> March 26, 1839. A lovely morning. Sat at home and wrote a third Psalm of Life, which I began long ago, but could never rightly close and complete till now. The beginning was written more than a year ago, and is copied under date of February 27, 1838; though, if I remember, I composed it a year earlier, even. In the afternoon I carried it to Felton [a friend who later became Harvard's first non-clerical

> president] and left it with him. He came up in the evening and said that he had read it to his wife, who 'cried like a child.' I want no more favorable criticism than this.

He titles his psalm "Footsteps of Angels." While composing it, Longfellow writes other poems, but not with the pastoral or battlefield themes he'd written as a boy. Instead, he searched his heart for inspiration. He writes:

> Look, then, into thine heart, and write!
> Yes, into life's deep stream
> All forms of sorrow and delight,
> All solemn Voices of the Night,
> That can soothe thee or affright,—
> Be these henceforth thy theme.

But grief throws a long shadow, and Longfellow continued to fight melancholy and despair. Remembering Goethe's doctrine—art is long, life is short, opportunity fleeting—he asked himself the following question to rally from depression:

> "What do I need to do, at this moment—"in the living present"—to live the life I was put on this planet to live?"

He remembered the graveyard at Salzburg. The words inscribed on the marble tablet on the chapel wall gave him the answer his heart needed:

> "Look not mournfully into the Past. It comes not back again. Wisely improve the Present. It is thine. Go forth to meet the shadowy Future, without fear, and with a manly heart."

He thought of the young nobleman buried beneath the tablet on the chapel's wall. From lips of dust, the dead young man had urged him to act in the living present, to live up to the best that is in him, to live a noble life.

Longfellow contemplated the testimony he'd received, a

manifesto from the dead to the living. He then transcribed the grave-side message into his poem, "The Psalm of Life," and he read it to his class at the close of a lecture on Goethe:

Trust no future, howe'er pleasant!
Let the dead past bury its dead!
Act, act—in the living Present!
Heart within, and God o'erhead!

He added the "Psalm of Life" to "Footsteps of Angels," and with Mary as his muse, Longfellow published his first volume of poetry, which he titles *Voices of the Night.*

The collection reflects the dual influence of Goethe and Novalis: the heroic call to fully live our lives despite deep sorrow and the strength found through remembrance of our beloved dead.

The public, well versed in grief and loss, responded in record numbers. Nine hundred copies sold in the first month, and four editions were printed within a year.

Longfellow's consolation poetry, forged from sorrow, touched his reader's hearts. *Voices of the Night* brought universal fame to the young college professor who would become the most popular author of his generation.

* * *

Longfellow's grief story had stunned me into silence.

I set aside the old, treasured books. After spending hours poring over volumes of biographies, journal entries, and poetry, I left the Portland Room of our public library in a daze.

I'd received my master's degree from Columbia University School of Social Work, and I'd interned at Memorial Sloan-Kettering, one of the finest oncology treatment centers in the world. For years, I'd worked as a clinical social worker and was considered an expert as I supported others through death, dying, and bereavement. Still, despite my training and experience, I didn't know how to live with my own grief.

The irony didn't escape me as I contemplated Longfellow's response to grief.

I'd been taught to separate and disconnect, but the young Longfellow, more than a century earlier, had successfully forged a different path. In his writing, he actually *promotes* a continued relationship with our beloved dead. I'd never before considered such a radical, alternate choice.

Could Longfellow possibly teach me new options for living with loss? Could what worked for him, work for me?

I had my doubts; I'd been taught to believe otherwise. But Longfellow's story gave me pause. It was time to explore other possibilities.

As I walked the streets of Longfellow's native town, my pace quickened.

How do we live with grief when it won't go away?

Maybe my question—at last—would be answered.

4

Footsteps of Angels

THE WORD "GRIEF" DERIVES FROM THE OLD French word *greve* meaning "heavy."

Heavy—that's how I felt as I staggered under the weight of loss. The heaviness compounded when I'd think of my brother who'd lost the person who knew him best, his partner and best friend. Then when I'd think of his young children who had no mother to dry their tears, I'd very nearly collapse.

I had nowhere to turn.

Feeling abandoned by God, I found no sustenance in faith, nor did my academic training provide consolation. It gave me knowledge about bereavement but not the strength to sustain me in my grief.

If anything, my professional background and its Freudian influence made grieving more difficult.

So much of the academic literature on bereavement reflects Freud's teaching about the grief process, as presented in his 1917 book *Mourning and Melancholia*.

Freud coined a word for emotional attachments that hold individuals together (such as spouse to spouse, parent to child, sibling to sibling). He called this act of bonding *cathexis*. The word is derived from the Greek word *kathexis* that means "to hold."

During our lifetime, according to Freud, our goal is to cathect through attachments and connection. During grief, our goal is to de-cathect through withdrawal of our attachments and disconnection. "Moving on" is the directive; holding onto our attachment is considered morbid.

Freud's essay branded grief as potentially pathological and led to later bereavement theories that label grief as an affliction the bereaved "must try to get over." Today, many clinicians continue to follow Freud's illness model and treat normal grief like a disease that requires medication.

Bereavement scholar Phyllis Silverman, among others, warns against this tendency to describe grief in pathological terms. Although grief can trigger an episode of depression for some individuals, she cautions us to consider "what it means when predictable, expected aspects of the life cycle experience are called 'disorders' that require expert care."

Nor is Silverman alone in her opposition. More recent clinical theories encourage providers to follow models of care that not only support continued connection but also allow for extended sadness.

Yet the illness model persists. We're still labeled "depressed" if we don't get over our sorrow.

It's not only professionals and their clients who feel Freud's influence; his teachings have been absorbed by our culture which endorses his concept of "letting go" and "moving on." In an ironic twist, Freud changed his perspective when faced with his own grief following the death of his daughter.

Thirteen years after his daughter died, Freud concedes that, although acute mourning passes, we can neither be consoled nor find a substitute after the death of a loved one. "And actually," he writes, "this is how it should be. It is the only way of perpetuating that love which we do not want to relinquish."

Although Freud changed his way of thinking, his original

thesis—to disconnect—remains the foundation for many grief therapies.

While working with cancer patients, I'd learned that disconnecting wasn't my strength, not when strong bonds had been formed. Dying is an intimate time. There are no strangers at a death bed, and I'd become close to the men and women who'd welcomed me into their sickroom. With each goodbye, my heart broke a little more until grief bowed me down.

My training had taught me to cope by withdrawing emotional attachments to my dear dead friends, but it gave me no guidance on how to live with my grief. Broken and burdened by sorrow, I left the field.

To cope with my sadness, I tried to marginalize my loss, but it didn't work. I soon learned that withdrawing emotional energy didn't annihilate my grief, it only tabled it. Then, when Sue died, new grief activated old grief and hurled me into the downward cycle of pain I'd long tried to avoid.

Emotional numbness came first.

In the blessed state of grief's initial shock, I managed to perform the sad tasks of the bereaved. I gave extra hugs to the children; I cooked and cleaned; I helped my brother plan the funeral; I made travel arrangements for my return to the States. I appeared stable, but it didn't last. When denial's numbing effect evaporated, grief threw me with tornado force into a spiral of suffering.

Although many cite the five stages of death and loss (denial, anger, bargaining, depression and acceptance), I knew better than to organize my moods into a tidy list. Long ago, while a social work intern at Memorial Sloan-Kettering, I'd learned that emotions neither recognized nor respected our revered stages.

Grief isn't that orderly. If only it was! We'd have less anxiety and more control. But there was nothing orderly about the anger, guilt, and fear raging through me. Instead of tidy, predictive stages to help me feel secure, grief's bedlam of pain left me fragile and exhausted.

However irrational, I blamed myself for Sue's death with a litany of "if only's." *If only* I'd gotten her into a research study, and she'd had more time with her children; *if only* I'd prayed with more faith, and a miracle had happened; *if only* I'd become an oncology doctor instead of an oncology social worker, and I'd found a cure for our Sue… *if only, if only, if only.*

I preferred to blame myself. It felt more stable to believe that I contributed to the cause of Sue's death rather than admit to things beyond my control. But self-blame didn't work. It provided only an illusion of control and proved no match for the grief that crushed me.

I tried to find respite through distraction. I took figure skating lessons, I rented movies, and I bought books, but nothing held my attention for long. I couldn't skate away, or laugh away, or read away my sorrow.

It looked like depression, but I knew from my training that it wasn't.

Unlike depression, normal grief has respite moments when the pain pauses, and I found temporary relief in the busy counseling practice I'd recently joined. Hour after hour, I'd meet with clients. Focusing on their concerns gave me respite from my own, but the relief was only temporary. At the end of the busy day, with the thrust of a surging wave, sorrow would knock me to my knees again.

Its force didn't surprise me. Aware of grief's fury, I'd expected emotional turbulence, but nothing prepared me for the private loneliness of grief. Even amid a group of people, I felt alone.

Concerned friends encouraged me to talk to someone, but why? A professional counselor would only direct me to disconnect, which I instinctively resisted.

Rather than face the deed of disconnecting, I avoided it. As I'd done with my hospital patients, I made myself less vulnerable to further pain by denying Sue's continued importance to me.

It seemed an easy solution. By sealing off my heart, I wouldn't have to consciously disconnect. It would happen by default. But I paid a high price for suppressing the love I held dear. Through disconnection, I deadened my soul and felt less alive.

Longfellow's poem suggests a different approach to loss. Instead of disconnecting, he keeps his attachment to his young bride. He doesn't deny Mary's death, but he doesn't deny her continued importance to him, either.

Longfellow's way seemed more appealing to me, but I was almost afraid to try it. To connect with a dead loved one—rather than disconnect—countered what I'd been taught as a student. The opposing viewpoints left me confused and undecided.

While considering Longfellow's position, I re-read "Footsteps of Angels," which triggered thoughts of Sue.

My mind flashed back to the sad moments following her death, when my brother pulled his sleeping bag and pillow to the nursery floor where Johnny and Alice lay sleeping. "I want to be with them when they wake up," he told me.

A few hours later, I could hear him tell his children the lead-heavy news. "Mummy died last night," he said.

Two-year-old Alice was too young to understand, but not four-year-old Johnny. "She can't be dead, Daddy," he protested. "She isn't very old yet."

I agreed with him. She was too young to die, but not even our most persuasive arguments could undo the tragic fact: she *was* too young, and she died anyway.

Throughout the morning, Johnny grappled with the truth. At one moment, he'd maneuver armored knights across the moat into their wooden castle, and in the next, he'd whimper,

"Mummy's dead." Then he'd blink back his tears, lower the drawbridge, and lead his brave toy men into battle.

Although Johnny could command his noble knights with complete authority, he was still a little boy who needed help getting dressed. I'll never forget the serious expression in his eyes as I buttoned his shirt and slid shoes onto his small feet.

"Auntie Gemma," he asked me as I tied his laces, "can you take me to see Mummy's body?"

He'd already seen her, but he wanted to see her again.

"Of course," I answered. Hand in hand, we approached the bedroom where Sue's body lay.

His little form froze by the bedside. Only his eyes moved, growing rounder and bigger as he stared at the stillness of his mother's face. I knelt beside him and repeated what his father had already told him.

"This is Mummy's body," I said softly. "She is no longer in it, Johnny."

He stared at her head and began to frown.

"But her whole body is here," I added, lest he magically think the rest of her had disappeared.

I lifted the sheets so he could see her body was intact.

"See, Johnny? Her whole body—not just her head—is here. And she's not hurting anymore."

He stared at the body of his mother, at once familiar and strange. He then turned his head toward the bedside table. Sue's glasses were still propped on a pile of books. Closer to the bed, an unfinished glass of water stood beside a framed photo taken a year earlier. He and Alice were posing in their Halloween costumes, embraced by a smiling Sue.

His mouth trembled downward as tears filled his eyes.

Dear, sweet Johnny! He could stoically examine a cold body, but the image of his loving mother, her arms around him, called up his greatest grief. He began to cry.

My brother responded with a father's instinct. His feet hardly touched the stairs, so swiftly did he fly into the room and lift the little boy into his arms.

Johnny cried against his shoulder while my brother held him close.

The little boy indicated the body on the bed. "That's Mummy," he sobbed.

"It's not Mummy," my brother gently told him, cradling the back of his head. "It's Mummy's body. Mummy isn't in it anymore."

"But I want her back in her body."

"So do I," my brother said.

He paced the room with Johnny in his arms and rocked him until the heaving stopped.

"She didn't want to go, Johnny," he told his young son. "She wanted to stay. But she just couldn't stay in her body anymore."

Johnny lifted his wet cheeks from my brother's shoulder. "Why couldn't she stay in her body?"

As though looking for an answer, my brother searched the room when he spotted a teacup and saucer perched on top of the dresser.

"Do you see that teacup, Johnny? Well, if there's a crack in the cup, if it's broken, it will not hold the tea. In the same way, Mummy's body was broken and could no longer hold her spirit."

Johnny looked at the teacup and then back at my brother. "But I want to talk to her," he said.

"You can still talk to her," my brother told him. "You can find new ways to talk to her."

The little boy shook his head. "But I don't know how to talk to her in a new way."

"It's true," his father replied, "You don't know how to talk to her yet. And neither do I. But I will learn new ways to talk to her, Johnny, and you will, too."

Johnny's hands moved in a flurry of questioning gestures. "But what if I can't learn a new way to talk to her?"

My brother answered at once.

"When you first came into this world, you didn't know how to talk to her, either, but you learned." He looked into his son's eyes. "And you will learn again."

My brother hadn't planned his words with his son, he later told me. Rather, he said, "something" had moved him to speak as he did; "something" had inspired him to not only recognize his continued attachment to Sue but to encourage his son to do the same.

At the time, I wondered, *could that "something" be Sue?* Could it have been Sue who told him what to say?

My relationship with Sue had grown in phases. There was the "getting to know you" phase. There was the phase when we let down our guard, and we began to trust each other. A joy-filled phase followed as love's energy connected us in a sister's bond. Then she died.

Freudian-influenced educators would tell me our relationship was over. You have no more phases to go through, they'd tell me. Don't hold onto the relationship. Disconnect and build new attachments. Get over it. Move on.

Longfellow, who believed Mary's affection for him remained unchangeable in life and in death, would disagree. Live wisely in the present, he would tell me, while continuing the attachment because the relationship is not over. It's simply entering a new phase.

But is there a phase in our relationship with loved ones that begins after death?

The cynic within me said "no." How could I believe that a relationship could continue after death? For years, I'd not felt God's presence, so how could I believe in a "sweet hereafter?" I wanted it. Who doesn't? But I couldn't believe it.

Others, smarter than I, believed it. C.S. Lewis in his own grief journal writes:

> (Death) is not a truncation of the process but one of its phases; not the interruption of the dance, but the next figure. We are 'taken out of ourselves' by the loved one while she is still here. Then comes the tragic figure of the dance in which we must learn to be still taken out of ourselves though the bodily presence is withdrawn, to love the very her…

To love the very her…to love the very Sue…

"We must find new ways to talk to her," my brother had been moved to say.

What if it *was* Sue who had inspired his counsel to their son? If so, might she also be near me, too? Could she possibly be waiting for me to initiate communication?

With guilt, I wondered if Sue, wanting to remain my big sister, could also be grieving and felt rejected when I froze her out.

Did my fear of another mournful collapse hurt her? Did my fear prevent a connection between us? Did my fear block my ability to love her? My head dropped in shame.

To love the very her… to love the very Sue…

Even if it was the most slight and remote possibility that Sue wanted to stay with me in my heart, who was I to deny her? To close her out would not be the way, as C.S. Lewis phrased it, "to love the very her."

We don't choose our losses, and I didn't choose to lose Sue. I didn't choose my fall into grief's dark pit, but I could choose my response to grief.

Now the road forked before me. Would I imprison myself in the comfort of my dark cell, shackled by fear? Or did I dare search for light in the darkness?

To open ourselves to spiritual possibilities—to a world unreachable by our intellect—requires an act of will, a decision to be open. But open to whom? To God? How could I trust God, when it was God who had sundered my heart's attachment?

For years, I'd felt abandoned by God. I'd tried to rationalize and force myself into acceptance, but nothing made sense. A loving God who abandons us was beyond my understanding.

"Strive not to understand that you may believe," St. Augustine once said, "but believe so that you may understand."

Aching with emptiness, I opened my closet door and considered the leather handbag that had once belonged to Sue. In an attempt to disconnect, I'd stashed it in a corner on the shelf.

But Freud's way hadn't worked for me; it was time to try something new. No more withdrawal of emotional attachments, I decided. No more busy avoidance and no more disconnection. Instead, I would follow Longfellow's example and invite Sue to "visit me once more."

Taking a deep breath, I pulled down the black purse and slung it over my shoulder.

"There are so many things to re-call the absent," writes Longfellow in a letter to a friend, "—the fragrance of a flower, a strain of music, a casual resemblance in voice, manner or feature; in fine, a thousand little things without a name, which suddenly startle me from my dream and make my pulses beat quicker."

As I smoothed my palms over the soft black leather of Sue's purse, my own pulse beat quicker. I then reached inside the bag and found an English penny in a zippered compartment. When my fingers held the coin that Sue had last held in hers, she startled me with her presence. The throbbing ache in my heart became still.

In that moment of presence—with penny in hand, purse by my side, and Sue in my heart—I received a message of hope for all who grieve and a way to find strength amid great sorrow.

— Part Two —

CONNECTION

"When the heart goes before, like a lamp and illumines the pathway, many things are made clear that else lies in darkness."

(from "Evangeline" by Henry Wadsworth Longfellow)

5

Connection to the Beloved

LONGFELLOW'S LIFE EXAMPLE BECAME MY master-class for living with grief. His first lesson transformed me.

Relationships don't end in death, he taught me, and as I opened myself to a connection with Sue, I began to know what Longfellow knew: The love between us never ends.

This is our good news. Although grief never goes away, *neither does the love.*

Longfellow never forgets his Mary. He finds romantic love again and enjoys domestic felicity with his second wife and their children, but he never forgets Mary. He couldn't have captured the ache of anticipatory grief in *Evangeline*, his epic poem about ethnic cleansing, without his personal story of love and loss.

In the final verse of his poem, Evangeline kneels beside her lover Gabriel as he lay dying. Like Longfellow at Mary's deathbed, Evangeline kisses Gabriel's lips as he dies in her arms:

> And as she pressed once more the lifeless head to her bosom, meekly she bowed her own, and murmured, 'Father I thank thee!'

The words uttered by Evangeline—"Father, I thank thee"—are the words spoken by Longfellow's young wife in her own final hours. Through his verse, he sanctifies Mary's memory, and through his continued connection with her, he reveals the love that does not end in death.

For many of us, continued connection can be a difficult concept to grasp. We're culturally indoctrinated to view connection with our departed beloved as pathological.

But this unfortunate mindset overlooks the distinction between healthy and unhealthy connection. Healthy connection, unlike its counterpart, is reality-based. It's not about living in the past, nor is it about denying the death of our loved one.

Longfellow never denied Mary's death. He fully experienced the pain of her loss, but he also remained connected with her. He didn't pretend she still lived; that wouldn't be a reality-based connection. Rather, he connected by recognizing the love between them that remained unchanged, in life and in death.

It never occurred to Longfellow to forget his beloved dead.

"Shall I thank God," he writes, "for all that makes this world so beautiful, and not for the good and beautiful beings I have known in it? Has not their presence been sweeter to me than flowers? Are they not higher and holier than the stars? Are they not more to me than all things else?"

Longfellow understood that, when we love someone, we are forever changed. Our loved ones, dead or alive, are part of us. To end our relationship—to forget them—is as unnatural as severing a limb from our body.

Nor do our loved ones want to be forgotten.

Mary Longfellow, as she lay dying, expresses the desire of the human heart. "Do not forget me," she whispered to Longfellow from her deathbed, and she speaks for all of us. After we die, we all want to be remembered by the people we love.

According to conventional wisdom, our goal in grief is to separate ourselves from our departed loved ones. We're supposed to end their influence over our lives by releasing our emotional and intellectual attachments to them.

But we who grieve know the protocol is flawed. Life doesn't *begin* following the death of a loved one, it *continues*, and detachment won't help us to endure. To live without our beloved requires significant strength—a strength that is attainable, not through detachment, but through connection.

Connection to our beloved—not detachment—provides the strength we need to go on.

As Longfellow demonstrates, our continued connection to their love for us gives us strength to endure the pain of loss. It gives us strength to get up in the morning although knowing, in Longfellow's words, "We shall not find in its accustomed place, the one beloved face." It gives us strength to go on.

But connection to our beloved is only part of our grief work. To honor our beloved, we need to do more.

Longfellow vowed, regardless of sorrow, to fully live his life. "This alone is health and happiness," he writes, "this alone is Life—Life that shall send a challenge to its end and, when it comes, say 'Welcome, friend!'"

We, too, can honor our loved ones by fully living our lives when we re-invest in life, and like Longfellow, connect with the love in the world that surrounds us.

6

Connection to the Love in the World

LONGFELLOW'S LIFE EXAMPLE ENCOURAGES connection with others, even when the heart is heavy. In the depths of grief, he "made the great friendships of his life," writes author Annie Fields, "of which he allowed no thread to break during the long years to come."

He'd often share his supper table and fireside with a friend. They would smoke a pipe into the early morning and "talk of matters which lie near one's soul, and how to bear one's self doughtily in life's battle, and make the best of things."

He reminded me of Eunice, a vibrant woman I knew through my work as an oncology social worker in a Philadelphia hospital.

I remembered how, like Longfellow, Eunice connected to the love in the world that surrounded her. Like him, she learned to bear herself "doughtily in life's battle and make the best of things."

A few weeks before her death from lung cancer, Eunice came to my office with a message to share.

"Gemma," she said, "the last two years have been the best two years of my life."

Then she told me something I'll never forget. "I've learned

how much I love," she said, "and how much I'm loved in return."

She leaned forward in her chair and flashed a broad grin. "Everyone should get cancer when they're twenty-one and be cured by the time they're twenty-two," she quipped. "The world would be a better place."

Although she had only days to live, Eunice had experienced connection with the love in the world surrounding her. No one on the planet radiated more joy.

Connection had transformed her.

Every Thursday, she attended a support group for cancer patients. At first, she didn't want to come. Her life-partner was a woman, and she expected the others would shun her. "They won't want me to be part of their group," she told me. But she somehow found the courage to attend, and to her surprise, she found unconditional acceptance.

During the first meeting, Eunice sat with the other members as they considered a name for their group. "Why not call our group "Surviving?" offered the youngest member. "Surviving," she added, "—that's what we do."

So they named their group *Surviving*, and that's what they did. Forging strong friendships, they survived together and supported each other through life and death.

Individually, they'd felt alone and frightened; together, they'd found new strength by replacing friendships they'd each lost to fear. Instead of competition, there was compassion, honesty, acceptance, and at the time of death, companionship.

In the presence of each other, they connected to the love in the world that surrounded them. This love between them didn't remove grief's pain—many of the group's members didn't physically survive their disease—but it gave them the strength to endure it.

It's not easy to extend our hand to another; fear can get in our way. Even an extrovert like Eunice, who'd feared rejection, had initially hesitated to reach out. But instead of letting fear isolate us from potential friends, we can be like Maggie, a spirited little girl I met on the playground.

Although Maggie was bald, she didn't let that stop her. Rather than hide in a corner sandbox, she joined the other children on the wooden play structure in the center of the park. After scaling its ladder and reaching the top platform, she extended her hand to every child within reach.

"Hi," she said with each handshake, "I'm Maggie. What's your name?" As she invited everyone to play with her, she became the pied piper of the playground.

"How old is Maggie?" I asked the slender woman who identified herself as Maggie's aunt.

"She's four," she answered.

My eyes fixed on the engaging creature. "She's amazing," I said.

The woman nodded, her eyes filling with tears. "She has leukemia," she told me. "She's in remission, but..." her voice faded.

The little girl didn't share her aunt's sadness, not at this moment. She was too busy making new friends and living life in the largest way.

Watching Maggie with her playmates, I realized that all of us can find strength in the midst of loss whenever, like Maggie, we connect with others. We are strengthened whenever, like Eunice and the members of the cancer support group, we know we're not alone.

Through connection to the love in the world that surrounds us, we can all find strength to live our lives—however long we have—with joy.

Longfellow celebrates such a connection in "The Arrow and the Song":

I shot an arrow into the air,
It fell to earth, I knew not where;
For, so swiftly it flew, the sight
Could not follow it in its flight.

I breathed a song into the air,
It fell to earth, I knew not where;
For who has sight so keen and strong,
That it can follow the flight of song?

Long, long afterward, in an oak
I found the arrow, still unbroke;
And the song, from beginning to end,
I found again in the heart of a friend.

Longfellow directs us to look upward, connecting with our beloved, *and* to look outward, connecting to the love in the world that surrounds us. Only one lesson from Longfellow remains: to look inward and connect to the divine-within.

7

Connection to the Divine-Within

TWO YEARS AFTER MARY'S DEATH, LONGFELLOW writes "A Psalm of Life."

He wrote his psalm, he later said, "from my inmost heart at a time when I was rallying from depression." In his psalm, he identifies what pulled him through—"Heart within, and God o'erhead"—and his courageous response to despair resonated with readers worldwide.

His poem inspired them to ask, "What action is life—'in the living present'—asking me to take?"

During the Crimean War, men recited "A Psalm of Life" as they lay dying on the battlefield; a student, who'd planned his suicide, changed his mind after reading it in class; and a grieving father, who anticipated the execution of his son during the Franco-German war, found the serenity to accept any fate after reading Longfellow's poem.

"I have been translating Longfellow's 'Psalm of Life,' and I am a new man," he told an American friend. "I feel that my mind is saved, and that faith and hope takes the place of despair. I owe it all to Longfellow."

From soldier to student to sorrowing parent, "A Psalm of Life" encouraged readers to embrace their noble spirit and to awaken the divine-within.

More than a century later, Austrian psychiatrist Victor Frankl, who would have studied the same German authors as Longfellow, alludes to "A Psalm of Life" in his book, *Man's Search for Meaning*, and re-states the poet's question that puts life in good order:

> "What action is life—in the 'living present'—asking me to take? What is life, at this moment, asking of me?"

Frankl, a Nazi concentration camp survivor, observed during his captivity that prisoners without meaning in their lives—without something to live for or hope for—would not likely survive. Like Longfellow, he recognized that noble pursuit, and not attainment, is the purpose of our existence.

"Mental health," he concluded, "is based on a certain degree of tension between what one has already achieved and what one still ought to accomplish, or the gap between what one is and what one should become.... We should not be hesitant about challenging man with a potential meaning for him to fulfill," he writes—even amid grief, depression, suffering, or imminent death.

According to Longfellow and Frankl, we find life's meaning by living the question, "What is life—at this moment—'in the living present'—asking of me?"

Kurt Messerschmidt, a cantor in Portland, Maine, lived that question.

Like Frankl, he survived captivity at a German concentration camp during World War II. His heroic story, presented in the *Portland Press Herald*, is a testament to faith, courage, and living a "psalm of life."

When Messerschmidt came of age, Europe was a threatening and dangerous place. But not even the anti-Semitic climate of post-World War I Berlin could discourage the idealistic teenager with the golden voice. He had a higher goal: to use his musical talent to bridge cultural differences through song.

But before he could apply his gift to heal the world, the Nazis came into power and thwarted his plan. Instead of performing musical diplomacy, Messerschmidt was deported to an infamous death camp where he worked in a quarry.

What did life, at that moment, ask of him?

It asked him to keep music alive in his heart, so he hummed.

While hauling heavy stones, he hummed his psalm. When it rained, with only a thin uniform to keep him dry, he still hummed. When it snowed, with only clogs to protect his feet from the wet chill, he praised God and kept on humming. Despite cold and hunger, he hummed from his heart and brought beauty to an ugly place.

It wasn't easy.

"It was a constant fight," Messerschmidt remembered. "I had to keep a separate inner life because they wanted to destroy my humanity, but they did not succeed."

It wasn't easy, but making music was what life, at that moment, required him to do. So he hummed, and his psalm became a song that saved lives.

One day, a suspected murderer, known for impulsively killing Jewish prisoners for stepping out of line, was assigned by the SS guards to supervise the prisoners' labor.

When Messerschmidt sensed the brute was ready to shoot someone, he began to hum.

As the young man's music filled the air, the thug came closer to listen. Liking what he heard, he ordered a work break so Messerschmidt could sing for him.

The future Cantor sang from the depths of his soul. As he sang, the brute, who'd threatened to slay the imprisoned men, remained by the work-camp's fireside, mesmerized by the beauty of the young man's voice.

As Messerchmidt sang, none of his fellow prisoners were

killed. As he sang, he saved lives.

Life had asked him to keep singing, and through his music, he opposed evil and hate with faith and love.

Like Longfellow before him, Messerschmidt kept "heart within and God o'erhead" throughout his imprisonment and the death march that followed, and no one could take it away from him. As he said, "They tried to take away my humanity, but they did not succeed."

By countering unholy hatred through connection to the divine-within, Messerschmidt created a separate inner life beyond the reach of earthly tyrants. It became his personal "Psalm of Life."

"Noble souls," writes Longfellow, "through dust and heat, rise from disaster and defeat the stronger, and conscious still of the divine within them, lie on earth supine no longer."

This power, "to lie on earth supine no longer," was well known to Dr. Elizabeth Kubler-Ross. As a pioneer in death and dying research, the compassionate doctor had witnessed the transformation of dying children when they connected to the divine-within.

I attended her lecture at Temple University in Philadelphia. I'll never forget the story she told us about her youngest patients on the hospital's pediatric ward.

"The children were afraid," she informed the rapt audience of health care providers.

Her patients were too young to understand the concept of death, Kubler-Ross explained, so she couldn't reach the source of their fear, nor could she soothe their anxiety. Her inability to help them frustrated her, but that changed following her journey to the Nazi concentration camps.

The Nazis murdered more than a million children during World War II. Kubler-Ross, long haunted by the slaughter of these innocents, made a special pilgrimage to honor them.

"I wanted to see where they kept the children before they died," she explained. So she traveled to the concentration camps at Auschwitz and Maidanek to visit the bunkers where the children awaited their death.

She expected to see the words "mommy" and "daddy" desperately scrawled on the walls, but she also saw an image that surprised her. On the walls in all the barracks, she found the image of a butterfly.

"Everywhere," she softly remarked, "I saw butterflies."

Somehow, the death-camp children had received an answer to Longfellow's essential question that awakens the divine-within:

> "What is life—at this moment—'in the living present'—asking of me?"

On the night before they died, these children knew what life asked of them.

Life asked them to learn from the butterfly breaking from the cocoon. Life asked them to look to the airborne creature and know that, at the time of death, the spirit within them, like the butterfly freed from its shell, will break through their body and fly. Life asked them to know that, although evil adults could murder their young bodies, they could not kill their souls.

In the doctor's hands, the butterfly markings became a gift of profound healing from these death-camp children to the pediatric patients on the cancer ward. Thanks to the boys and girls who left butterflies behind them, Kubler-Ross could now explain death to her young patients and expel their anxiety.

She surveyed her audience of doctors, nurses, and social workers. "So now when I visit the dying children," she told us, "I bring this puppet."

She reached into a bag and pulled out the facsimile of a cocoon, sewn from black fabric. Then she lifted the puppet to the podium and told us the story she would tell her young patients about the cocoon and the butterfly.

The cocoon, she would instruct them, is a temporary dwelling for the butterfly. In time, the cocoon ruptures and cannot be fixed. That's when the butterfly is released.

From the lecture hall podium, Kubler-Ross inserted her hand into the body of the puppet and raised her arm. She worked the folds of the black fabric, and as the multicolored wings of a butterfly broke through the black velvet cocoon, she fluttered the wings in the air.

She then told us what she would tell the children. "You are like the butterfly, and your body is like the cocoon," she'd explain. "And just as the broken cocoon can no longer hold the butterfly, there comes a time when your body can no longer hold you—your spirit—your true self.

"When the cocoon gets broken and cannot be fixed, the butterfly is released. And like the cocoon, when our bodies are broken and cannot be healed, we die. When we die, our own butterfly—our true self—is released."

She would then pass the puppet, in cocoon form, to her young patients and invite them to slide their hands into the puppet's cavity. She would watch as the children worked the folds of the fabric to release the butterfly. She would wait for them to behold the splendor of the puppet in flight. Then, as they flew their butterfly through the air, she would share the message she'd received from the children at Auschwitz and Maidanek.

"And when *you* die," she would tell her young patients with the soaring puppet in their hand, "*you* will be beautiful, like the butterfly."

When Kubler-Ross finished her story, she paused, as though to emphasize what we needed to replicate in our own work.

She looked on her audience with a serene expression. "Now when I talk to the dying children," she told us, "they understand and are no longer afraid."

They were no longer afraid because the image freed them to soar like the butterfly, conscious of the divine-within.

* * *

We, too, can become conscious of the divine-within when, like Frankl and Messerschmidt, we live Longfellow's essential question that is our gateway to the internal:

> "What is life—at this moment—'in the living present'—asking of me?"

When we live that question, we uncover our own psalm of life. By living our own psalm of life, we're led to the divine presence within.

This sacred connection to the divine-within transforms us. It fortifies, purifies, and perfects us; and as the children of the holocaust taught the children on the cancer ward, it conquers fear of all things, even death.

8

Grief Work, Connection, and the Power of Consolation

THERE IS NO GRIEF, WRITES LONGFELLOW, LIKE the grief that does not speak, and the time comes for all of us to suffer and be silent.

But how can we endure grief so unutterable that we cannot speak of it? How can we bear the dark night of the sorrowing soul? How can we go on?

Longfellow asked these questions and lived his way to the answers. We can find our way when we follow his lead.

Nineteenth-century Scottish minister Henry Drummond provides initial instruction. "Effects require causes," he writes.

The world is methodical, he explains. If someone bakes a good cake, it's the result of a sound recipe, carefully applied. The baker brings ingredients together and sets causes at work; these causes bring about the result.

Random causes don't produce specific effects any more than random ingredients produce specific cakes.

"So it is," Drummond writes, "in the making of human experience. Certain lines are followed, certain effects are the result. But the result can never take place without the previous cause. To expect results without antecedents is to expect cakes without ingredients."

When we apply Drummond's instruction to grief and follow his cause and effect formula, we begin to know what Longfellow knew, and we begin to understand what can help us through our own dark night.

Because we've loved and lost (cause), we grieve (effect). It's the saddest of causes producing the saddest of effects. Our grief then becomes a cause for the downward spiral of emotional pain that nothing can stop.

It's in this place of deep pain that our need is clarified: We need comfort.

The word *comfort* derives from the French language and means "with strength," and that's what we need. We've been thrown overboard into a frigid, heaving sea, and we need something strong and solid to bring us to shore. We need comfort—or strength—to endure grief's unending pain.

So if strength is the effect we seek, what is its cause? If consolation means "that which gives comfort" or "that which strengthens," how can we find strength and realize consolation for our grieving hearts?

Professor Drummond reminds us about cause and effect. So what can we do (cause) to find the strength (effect) we need to go on?

Longfellow—and the courageous men, women, and children remembered in these pages—lived the answer in one, imperative word: "*Connect!*"

They show us three powerful ways to connect: connection to our beloved, connection to the love in the world that surrounds us, and connection to the divine-within.

It's a "cause and effect" method. When we connect (cause), we receive the strength to carry sorrow's heavy load that brings consolation to the grieving heart (effect). When we connect, consolation follows.

But we first need to connect. Connection is our grief work.

Connection then graces us with consolation by providing the strength to live with grief that doesn't go away.

Whether living in the nineteenth century or the twenty-first, it presents a powerful blueprint for living with grief.

The following "cause and effect" guidance can help support the strength-giving consolation that sustains us in our grief:

1. SET ASIDE TIME FOR PRIVATE AND SOCIAL ACTIVITIES

Disorder and confusion follows loss, but a structured routine brings external order that can contain the chaos of grief. Even when our energy is low, it can be helpful to schedule activities to help restore our balance.

Private activities such as prayer, yoga, writing, art, music, reading, poetry, or exercise can become a meditative expression of our deepest longing, regenerating the body while restoring the soul.

Public pursuits such as classes, sports, lunch dates, clubs, shared meals, concerts, movies, and theater can become an outward expression of re-investment in life.

There's no limit to what we can add to this list; any activity that brings vitality will serve. But don't underestimate the importance of scheduling both private and social time when deep in bereavement. We need to pursue all possibilities that can recharge us—body and soul—with the needed strength to endure our grief.

2. INVITE INNER QUIET

The time comes for all of us, writes Longfellow, to suffer and be silent. But silence is not only the absence of sound. Silence is also the quieting of our chattering inner voice.

Breathing deeply can center us. Reflective writing, reading, meditation, or prayer can help to still the noise that stimulates our brains. The resulting inner quiet can help us listen with new awareness to the fullness of life that surrounds us.

Longfellow called sorrow "our little school masters." When we quiet our own voice, the profoundness of pain can lead us—as it led Longfellow—to listen more closely to the wisdom of the ages that teaches the heart and sustains the soul.

3. ENGAGE IN LIFE

We find strength whenever, in the midst of loss, we seek life. We renew the life force within when, like Longfellow, we choose not to isolate but to engage.

Longfellow's deepest grief taught him to appreciate the wisdom of Horace. He often quoted the *Ad Thaliarchum:*

> "What may the morrow be, shun thou to question. What e'er the days may bring, make thou the best of it. Spurn not, O boy, the sweet loves, nor the dances."

4. TAKE ACTION

We uncover strength as we maximize our potential to be, each moment of each day, the person we were put on earth to become.

From our place of reflection, we can develop an "action plan of meaning" by asking three questions:

1. How can I connect to my beloved dead, to the world around me, and to the divine-within?
2. What does life, at this moment, ask of me?
3. What can I do today to follow through?

The answers to these questions guide us with a plan. Consolation—that which gives strength—comes as we follow our action plan.

"Act! Act!" writes Longfellow, "in the living present." His "Psalm of Life" was his own vow to live more conscientiously.

We, too, can write and live our own psalm of life. It's a powerful antidote to despair.

5. FOCUS ON THE PHYSICAL

We live in the world and in our bodies.

Connection to our physical surroundings—and all living forms within it—restores energy depleted by grief. We find renewed strength whenever we connect with breathing beings, human and animal, and when we cultivate our living space or plant life in the earth.

We also need to mind the body. When tears fill our eyes, we must find a private place to let ourselves cry. When grief exhausts our body, we must take it to bed. When our body is restless, it helps to give it something to do: take a walk, go for a run, enjoy a swim, ride a bike. When our body is hungry, we must feed it.

We need marathon strength for grief, and when we meet our physical needs and connect to our physical world, we unearth new energy to help us endure.

6. ABSORB THE NATURAL WORLD

We receive beauty when we use our five senses—touch, sight, taste, smell, hearing—to experience nature's wonder and absorb the world that surrounds us.

We can also use our five senses to re-imagine, in our mind's eye, a place from our past where beauty filled us with wonder. Through sense memory, we can then choose to remember details of our special space and re-enter it at will.

Only by taking the time to go to a beautiful place—real or imagined—can we receive nature's gift of peace and solace. The beauty of the natural world, when we allow it to surround us, can shelter us from stress, replenish the spirit, and soothe the grieving soul.

7. PLAY

We can uncover hidden strengths by doing something from our youth. What we enjoyed once, we can enjoy again.

An exploration of past experiences brings an unexpected benefit: When we mine our past for playful activities, we can uncover our true nature, before responsibilities masked joys that were once obvious and attainable.

Examine all past activities to help determine potential activities for the present. Consider participating in a sport; making music; playing card games or board games; building a model airplane, ship, or vintage car; painting a picture; taking a class; stringing a necklace; finishing a puzzle. With the openness of the younger self, re-discover favorite activities such as walking or skating; riding a bike; singing, dancing, and drawing; sewing and writing; creating; baking; and cooking.

We need not be limited to pleasures from our past. We also find strength when we try something new and make fresh discoveries about ourselves and our world.

8. READ AND WRITE WITH CARE

Longfellow found it "exquisite to read good novels in bed with wax candlesticks."

Like Longfellow, we can read novels, poems, or philosophical essays. We can write down feelings in a journal or in a letter to a friend.

Do be cautious with the material. Longfellow warns us to pay attention to what we put in our "brain pan," as he calls it. Avoid anything toxic, anything upsetting. Strength comes through connection, not distress.

9. ACCEPT THE CHANGING NEEDS OF GRIEF

Sometimes we need to cry. Thousands of years ago, Aristotle observed the human need for catharsis provided by the plays of ancient Greece.

Sometimes we need to laugh. In the depths of tragedy, Shakespeare placed his clowns.

In the history of theater, tragedy came first, and comedy followed. Like the ancient playwrights, we can balance our sadness with moments spent in a lighter mood. Humor provides a welcome break that helps sustain us in our grief.

10. RECEIVE THE BLESSINGS OF OTHERS

In the months following the crib-death of her baby daughter, sorrow often startled my mother out of her bed.

During the awful loneliness of one early morning—her empty arms heavy with loss—consolation surprised her when she remembered a fact told by a priest during a college class she'd taken years earlier:

> At all times of the day and night—somewhere in the world—monks and nuns are at prayer, kneeling in solidarity for all who suffer.

As she remembered and pondered his words, she bowed her head with all who prayed for her. In that pre-dawn hour, she felt the power of their prayer. And at that moment, cradled by their care, the young bereaved mother received the consolation she needed to go on.

Like my mother, we find strength whenever, from that deep-beneath-us place, we join the stream of unconsciousness inhabited by these contemplatives. Here, where soul meets soul, we are never alone.

* * *

Consolation doesn't always take the form we expect, nor does it always appear when we're looking for it. We need only keep a receptive heart, and as Longfellow guides us, mindfully move toward connection—connection with our beloved, connection with the love in the world that surrounds us, and connection to the divine-within.

We need only connect. When we connect, consolation *will* find us, soothe us, inspire us, and give us the inner strength to live with joy again.

— Part Three —

CONSOLATION

"The sky is filled with stars, invisible by day."

(from "Morituri Salutamus" by Henry Wadsworth Longfellow)

9

The Fullness of Melancholy

IN GRIEF'S FIRST MOMENTS, THE DEATH OF OUR loved one stuns us with shock.

This initial numbness allows us to perform necessary tasks. We manage to take care of children while making funeral arrangements and telephone calls. We go to the grocery store and prepare our meals. We pay our bills. We get to work on time.

"Aren't they doing well?" people say about us, but we're operating on auto-pilot, and it doesn't last. Soon—and without warning—grief pummels us with hurricane force.

"The swelling heart heaves moaning like the ocean," observes Longfellow, "that cannot be at rest."

We find, like Longfellow, that without shock to shield us from grief's great fury, we're battered by waves of anger, depression, and fear that throw us to the ground and drain our energy.

"I loathe the slightest effort," notes C.S. Lewis after the death of his wife.

Brittle and exhausted, we find that nothing can obliterate the heartache, not even activities we've enjoyed in the past.

Like Lewis, we crave medicine to make it better. "What am I to do?" he writes in his journal. "I must have some drug, and reading isn't a strong enough drug right now."

There are short respite moments when the pain pauses. We notice we can share a joke with a friend, enjoy an article in a magazine, or escape into a television episode. The reprieve, however pleasant, is only temporary. Sorrow always returns and knocks us to our knees with shattering force.

"How long can this last?" we ask.

Lewis fearfully adds, "Will it be for always?"

"How long," cries the biblical psalmist, "shall I harbor sorrow in my soul, grief in my heart, day after day?"

With time, grief's painful surges become less powerful. The lull between swells of anguish becomes longer in duration until the waves of pain subside, and we can rest.

But we mustn't be fooled; it isn't over. Not yet, not ever. Grief comes back. Even after decades have passed, a sense memory can recall our beloved so vividly, that it throws us to the ground with the force of grief's initial power.

Anything can re-open the wound: a Christmas tree ornament, a lingering scent from a sweater, an anniversary, a voice, a familiar face or object, the words to a song. The most trifle is enough to stir the broken heart.

But unlike the early days of our grief, the duration of acute distress in later grief is brief. A dull ache soon replaces the shooting pain, and once again, the long lull between the waves of grief returns. Another temporary reprieve begins.

It can be helpful—when dazed by the ebb and flow of grief—to know that our tidal waves of emotion are normal. It helps to know we're not going crazy. But knowledge alone isn't enough to sustain us.

Only connection can bring us to safe harbor. Only through connection can we find consolation.

So what if we do everything in our control to prepare for strength-giving consolation—we connect to our beloved, to the love in the world that surrounds us, and to the divine-within—and consolation doesn't come? We've done all the work, and nothing happens? Instead of peace found through connection, we ache and feel hollow inside. What then?

It helps to remember that grief must have its way.

After a physical injury, physical therapy rebuilds the body's strength, but it doesn't eradicate pain. In the same way, connection gives us the strength to endure grief, but as Longfellow experienced, it doesn't eliminate the suffering.

"I sometimes think," he writes, "that no one with a head and a heart can be perfectly well."

The grief following Mary's death was compounded by Fanny's initial rejection of his marriage proposal. The combined loss and heartbreak nearly broke his health, yet Longfellow never stopped connecting. Volumes of letters attest to it. Even when stunned by grief, he remained connected.

Longfellow writes that we mustn't give up nor be impatient, but "learn to labor *and to wait.*"

Grief is a lengthy process, and it may take years to work through it. But in time, Longfellow tells us, lightness will fill our innermost being. It can seem so sudden, it's often experienced as an "awakening," although the seeds for serenity have long been planted. He writes:

> In the life of every man, there are sudden transitions of feeling, which seem almost miraculous. At once, as if some magician had touched the heavens and the earth, the dark clouds melt into the air, the wind falls, and serenity succeeds the storm. The causes which produce these sudden changes may have been long at work within us; but the changes themselves are instantaneous, and apparently without sufficient cause.

Our work isn't to feel the "serenity that follows the storm," but to implement the cause for it. Consolation—that which strengthens us—will come if we lay the groundwork.

Our imperative is to connect to the beloved, to the love in the world that surrounds us, and to the divine-within. Only connect, and in time, "the dark clouds melt into the air." Only connect, and in time, serenity will follow.

We must be patient. Strength-giving consolation comes through the process of connection, and like knowledge, we acquire it slowly. We need only keep our hearts open and receptive so we may both recognize and receive it when it comes.

It's difficult to believe consolation will find us when we feel nothing but sorrow.

"I'm like water poured out," laments the biblical psalmist, "all my bones are racked."

When pain stabs with such severity, it's hard to imagine anyone else suffers what we do, like the woman in this Buddhist story:

> There was a mother whose child had died. Overcome with grief, she carried the dead body of her son to the Buddha. All others in her family had died, and her boy was all that remained.
>
> "O, great teacher and master, please bring my child back to life," she pleaded.
>
> The Buddha gently looked upon her. "Bring me a mustard seed from a family in the village that has not experienced loss," he said, "and I will bring back your child."
>
> The mustard seed was the most common spice in India, so when the mother accepted the Buddha's task, she expected she would easily succeed.
>
> She returned to her village and began her pilgrimage from house to house. But as she knocked on each door, she sadly discovered that each family had a story of loss to tell, and every household had experienced death.
>
> The mother wept with sorrow. She could not bring a mustard seed to her great teacher, and her child would not—as she had hoped—be brought back to life.

Through tears, she faced the sad fact: all who are born will also die, and those who love will also grieve.

In this place of resignation, one of Longfellow's friends, desolate after the death of his young wife and infant son, asked the poet to translate the German poem, "Two Locks of Hair."

The last two stanzas, translated by Longfellow, bluntly address the melancholy and despair of grief:

> Two locks—and they are wondrous fair—
> Left me the Vision mild;
> The brown is from the mother's hair,
> The blonde is from the child.
>
> And when I see that lock of gold,
> Pale grows the evening red!
> And when the dark lock I behold,
> I wish that I were dead.

It may seem odd that Longfellow's bereaved friend would consider this poem a source of consolation. "Wanting to be dead" is not a sentiment we dare admit, but it's how we feel when a loved one dies.

When we accept our melancholy and acknowledge that others share this despondency, we begin to understand the universality of grief. In our suffering and sadness, we are neither odd nor alone. Longfellow writes:

> Such ploughshares do not go over us for naught; they turn up the deepest parts of our natures and make us more akin to all who have suffered.

It leads us to the paradox of grief.

In our anguished sorrow and seeming alone-ness, we are most one with the human family. In the lonely depths of darkness, we join people of all races, ethnic backgrounds, and religious faiths. In the profundity of individual pain, we meet people who live now, who've lived before us, and who have yet to be born.

In the fullness of melancholy, not one of us is alone. Here, we enter the heart of suffering humanity where, like Longfellow's bereft friend, we can connect with the universe and find consolation.

10

Consolation Surrounds Us

GOD IS IN THE SPACE BETWEEN PEOPLE, TEACHES Jewish theologian Martin Buber.

That's where we find strength-giving consolation: in the space between us and our beloved, the space between us and the love in the world, and the space between us and the divine-within. This sacred space-between holds all relationships. The space between us—this divine space—transforms our suffering and makes it something new.

The Irish poet and philosopher John O'Donohue describes this sacred space between us as "a secret climate of profound kindness that sends us bouquets of light and color when we experience forlorn times."

Consolation, realized through the love found in the space between us, gives strength to the grieving heart. I now realize that I'd been receiving consolation all my life to help me cope with grief.

I remember how I felt years ago when Margo, the youngest member of our cancer support group, died.

Disoriented by grief, I stumbled in a stupor through the market as I shopped for my dinner. When I dropped my items on the checkout counter and opened my wallet, I discovered a lack of dollar bills. These were the days before debit cards, and without paper money to pay for my groceries, I'd have to leave them at the counter and forgo my dinner.

"That will be $9.57," the cashier said.

I pulled out the dollar bills and added them fast. As I suspected, I fell short. Then I counted every coin in my purse. To the penny, I had *exactly* $9.57.

What are the odds? I felt my jaw drop in surprise.

"Margo!" I said to myself as I felt her presence. Through a sensed connection with Margo, I received consolation in a checkout line.

I also received consolation after my friend Tom died.

For months before he died, we'd talk and laugh; for months after he died, I cried. One morning, after weeks of missing him, I slipped into a jacket I hadn't worn in a long time and found, folded in a pocket, a piece of paper torn from a pink pad. My heart lurched as I skimmed the words scrawled across the page.

"Tom called," it read. "Call anytime."

He'd left the phone message for me weeks earlier, but now—after his death—it held new meaning.

Call anytime.

So I decided to call on him. "Be with me, Tom," I urged.

He answered me—not verbally—but soul-to-soul. From the same deep-beneath me place where I'd felt his absence, I now felt flooded with his presence. Waves of warmth alternated with goose flesh chills as I carefully re-folded the paper and returned it to my pocket.

My connection with Tom—as potent as a face-to-face meeting—re-united me with my friend and gifted me with strength-giving consolation.

In the novel *Harry Potter and the Prisoner of Azkaban,* the wizard Dumbledore discusses the power of consolation received through continued connection with our beloved dead.

He tells the young Harry how our dead loved ones never truly leave us. "Your father is alive in you, Harry," the wizard tells the boy, "and shows himself most plainly when you have need of him."

All of us can follow the words of the wise wizard, and when we're very low, watch for our loved ones who are alive in us. Sometimes we need a child-like faith to see.

One morning, when my daughter was six, I heard her happily chatting in the backseat of the car. "Who are you talking to? I asked with a mother's curiosity.

"Auntie Sue," she replied.

"Auntie Sue?"

"Oh, yes," she said, "I'm talking to the Auntie Sue who died."

"Is she saying anything to you?" I couldn't help but ask.

My daughter upbraided me with her reply. "Mommy," she said, "it's not about that. It's about the *presence.*"

With a child's innate wisdom, she enlightened me. Connection isn't a message, an intervention, or a physical sign; these are conduits for connection but not connection itself. Rather, connection—and the consolation that follows—is the ongoing presence of love between us that doesn't end in death.

We're fortunate that consolation received through connection isn't limited to times of deep trouble or danger. Nor must we wait for our beloved to connect with us; we can initiate connection ourselves. Even obligations can be become an opportunity to connect, as demonstrated by my friend Marge.

After moving from Pennsylvania to Maine, Marge needed a new driver's license, but she had to take a written test before she could get it. Although she knew she'd pass—she had years of experience behind the wheel—she delayed the date for the exam.

"I waited for the right day to do it," she later told me.

Her father had taught her how to drive, and on the

anniversary of his birth, she made her decision. "This is the day I will take my test," she told herself, "because Daddy will be proud of me."

Strengthened by the father-daughter relationship that doesn't end in death, Marge made her way to the Motor Vehicles Department where she took the driving test, and on her father's birthday, she passed it.

Our five senses can become another gateway to connection-based consolation.

My friend Bill recounted his visual consolation experience following the funeral of his father, a World War II hero decorated with a purple heart, a silver star, and a bronze star.

"I was sad but happy because Dad really missed Mom," he told me. "They were a handsome couple, and he truly missed her. It had been eleven years since she passed."

His mother, he remembered, had a knack for gathering four-leaf clovers. "She'd focus in and find them," he recalled.

So Bill, like his mother, would look for four-leaf clovers in the grass. While walking down Deering Street after his dad's funeral, he thought, "I haven't seen a four-leaf clover in a while."

His eyes darted to the tufts of grass beside the sidewalk. "Right there," he said, "on the edge of the pavement, there was the *biggest* four-leaf clover, and I said, 'Thanks, Mom!'"

Then Bill, the oldest of five children, received a second consolation. Behind the big clover in the grass, he spotted five more four-leaf clovers.

"One for each of us kids," he marveled while collecting the symbols to share with his siblings.

"The first one was about Mom," he said, "but when I saw *five*, I knew Mom and Dad were together."

Some people, like Diane, receive consolation through the sense of smell. After her father died, she'd often detect the scent of his after-shave. "I'd smell his 'Old Spice,'" she told me, "and I'd know he was with me."

Others, like Rachel, receive consolation through the sense of hearing.

Six months after the death of her brother, she canoed down the Saco River with her husband. As they paddled through the ice-cold rapids, she heard the incessant cawing of a crow.

The harsh sound initially irritated her, but as the crow stalked them down the river, she soon feared for their survival. The crow loomed low over them as they crossed the river's most treacherous stretch. Then, when the waters calmed, the crow suddenly vanished. That's when Rachel realized the crow had followed her only while she was in danger and had disappeared only when she was safe.

"I know it sounds strange," Rachel recalled, "but my brother was always a protector, and that crow made me feel like my brother was with us and protecting us."

At that moment of presence, when she realized the loving space-between them had remained intact, Rachel received the deep consolation of her brother's love that did not end in death.

We can also use sense memories to cultivate a habit of connection, like Edwina who uses a breakfast ritual to keep her mother close.

"My mother always loved her marmalade and toast," she told me. To commemorate her mother, Edwina now enjoys the same breakfast treat on Sunday mornings and spreads marmalade on her own piece of toast. The weekly routine—the smell, the taste, the ritual—activates a vivid remembrance that keeps her mother near.

We can also, like Deb, cultivate a habit of connection through activities of daily living. Deb recalled how her mother, who died a few years ago, had often found bliss through the solitary ritual of a relaxing bath. So now, whenever Deb takes time for herself through a bath-time ritual, she experiences her own bliss as she thinks of her mom and senses her presence.

We can also connect with loved ones through objects, like Longfellow did. In his early grief, he kept a little bronze chapel always on his table. Given to Mary as a souvenir, it reminded him of the happy days they shared.

Even an object that provokes anxiety can be a source of connection and consolation.

My grandmother, who died several years ago, had crocheted afghan blankets for each of her grandchildren. During her lifetime, whenever I wrapped myself in her blanket, I felt her warmth around me, but after she died, the blanket made me anxious.

What if I stained it? What if moths bore holes into the wool? Above all else, I worried about losing it. Would it be like losing my grandmother a second time?

Then I realized that losing the blanket couldn't end my love for my grandmother, nor could it end her love for me. Nothing could unravel the fabric of our love, not even death.

The blanket served a purpose, much like a beloved toy that helps a child feel safe when away from home. In time, it's no longer needed. For me, the blanket was a transitional object that, in my early grief, helped me to cultivate a habit of connection with my grandmother that will never end.

There are many ways to deliberately seek connection with our beloved and receive consolation. Sometimes we need only to ask, and we receive it.

One night, I couldn't sleep. I tried progressive relaxation exercises, and I counted sheep backwards, but nothing worked. Soon I began to feel pressured. I knew my daughter, who was four at the time, would wake early, and I'd need all my energy in the morning.

After relentless tossing, I felt desperate. I turned to my beloved grandfather who'd died when I was ten.

"Pompa," I asked, "please stay with me through the night."

It was my last conscious thought before falling asleep. I didn't wake until I felt a whisper in my ear, followed by audible words.

"Goodbye," it said. It wasn't my husband's voice, but it sounded pressured and had a robotic monotone.

I looked immediately at my husband's pillow. He wasn't there. I noted the time on the digital clock, "6:00 a.m.," and instinctively glanced toward the doorway. In the twilight state between dreaming and waking, I saw the shaded form of a man. I couldn't see his features, but a diffuse light outlined the shape of his felt hat and the strong lines of his shoulders.

It was the unmistakable presence of my grandfather. I knew him at once. From that deep-beneath-me place where true knowledge resides, I knew him. With the clarity of consolation, he'd come to me in the night as I'd requested, and left me with an awe-based strength to face the day.

Such visitations can seem too "other worldly" to be real, so we deny their actuality. "It's only a dream," we say. But such a dismissal blocks a powerful opportunity to connect to the love between us.

Whether such visitations are real or imagined isn't the point. What matters is the love between us manifested by these visitations and the strength we receive through that love.

Sometimes connection to our beloved can be realized through happenstance. The following incident occurred on Longfellow's wedding anniversary to Fanny (also the date of her funeral). He found it so remarkable that he recorded it in his journal. He writes:

> Ah, those melancholy anniversaries! I was awakened this morning about sunrise by the singing of a bird inside my room. I looked up and saw it perched on the window-blind. It then hopped into the room,—a little yellow

bird with brown wings. After singing awhile, it perched on the rounds of a chair, then flew out of the other window.

We often dismiss such happenings as mere coincidence, like one of my clients who shared her consolation story following the death of her father.

She'd found a penny on a sidewalk, minted the year of her father's birth. She'd felt enormous comfort on seeing her dad's birth year stamped on the coin, she told me, although she felt somewhat sheepish telling me about it.

"It's probably nothing," she shrugged, "just a coincidence."

At the time, ignorant about the cause and effect of connection and strength-giving consolation, I would have nodded in agreement. Today, I would counsel her differently. I would tell her about strength-giving consolation, and how it often works through coincidence.

Consolation—the strength we receive when we connect to the love between us—can be found in the smallest of things. We can find it in a telephone message, a checkout line, a familiar scent, a four-leaf clover, a crow, or even in a penny. We can find it in the comfort of friends. We can find it in a movie, a TV show, a song, a symphony, or a book. We can find it in a memory, an activity, a dream, a bird, a butterfly, a pet, or a poet.

Consolation's power lies—not in our sensory experience of an activity, object, or image—but in the love between us that does not end in death. The activity, object or image calls forth that love, as a photo recalls a face. The love realized through this connection is the consolation we seek, and we receive it through any sign in our world that connects us to our beloved.

Consolation, when observed by others, may seem insignificant and small in stature. It may seem so small, we don't recognize it ourselves. But when we pay close attention and watch with new eyes, we can both recognize and receive it.

Love doesn't end in death. Although unseen, love is between us, it surrounds us, and it's within us. We need only connect to this love, and consolation will follow.

11

Choices

CONSOLATION—THAT WHICH GIVES US STRENGTH—is everywhere, all the time. Even in the heavy haze of early grief, consolation can illuminate our darkened heart chamber.

But it's not always easy to receive consolation. It exposes us to vulnerability, and many of us prefer to ignore it. Ted's story offers a different choice.

I met Ted years ago, during my practice as an oncology social worker.

"Life is a beach," read the hand-scrawled sign on his hospital door. "Nurses please enter in bikinis."

As I made my rounds down the corridor of the cancer unit, I'd often hear laughter when I passed his room. Nurses left his bedside with a bounce in their step, and doctors smiled as they mentioned his name.

I was new at the hospital. I didn't yet know his medical history, so I assumed his high spirits reflected an excellent prognosis. My assumptions, however, were incorrect. I soon learned this remarkable man had leukemia, and his prognosis was poor.

He perplexed me. Ted was only thirty-five years old and happily married with school-aged children. He had every reason to be angry, depressed, and fearful. Instead, he exhibited acceptance, joy, and serenity.

How did he manage it? What did he know that the rest of us didn't?

Every day, suffering and sadness surrounded me. If he could tell me how to attain joy in the face of death, maybe he could, through me, enlighten others.

I'll never forget the afternoon I met with him. He lay sideways on his hospital bed, ready to tell his story.

"What's your secret, Ted?" I asked. "Other people need to know it."

His smile reached his eyes. "I'll tell you," he said.

He indicated his large body. "I didn't always look like this. I used to go to the gym. I had toned muscles. But after I got sick, my muscles turned to fat."

He then pointed to his head, bald from chemo. "And I used to have lots of hair."

He spoke without self-pity. In fact, he glowed as he spoke, almost as though he preferred his new self. His voice became more animated as he detailed his own struggles with depression.

"I used to be a great looking guy. Then I became fat and bald, and I became afraid. I thought, 'I'm so ugly, my wife can't possibly love me.' I then became convinced of it. The thought she didn't love me made me hurt, angry, and depressed. I didn't talk to her for days."

At this point in his story, he paused as if to savor the contrast of his current mood with his past emotions.

I didn't want to rush him. I tried to curb my curiosity, but I couldn't wait to hear his secret. How did this man move from fear to serenity, from desolation to joy?

"What happened," I asked, "that changed it for you?"

Propping himself up on his elbow, he rested his cheek on his hand as a sweetly tender expression crossed his face. "I'll tell you what changed it for me," he said. "My wife brought me a rose."

On first hearing his response, I was dissatisfied. How could his answer help the other patients on the oncology floor? I'd hoped for a tidy formula I could share with them, but his answer baffled me. It was too simple. Where were the details about his process that could transform all of us? What was the secret to his success?

I tried not to sound incredulous as I heard myself repeat his words. "Your wife brought you a *rose*?"

His eyes widened. "Yes," he answered, "My wife brought me a rose. It's as simple as that."

As he continued, he slowed his speech so that I could better comprehend the meaning of his message. "At that moment, I knew—I *knew*—she loved me." He punctuated his statement with a pause. "She loved me, and that made all the difference."

He relaxed his body back onto his side and nestled his cheek into his pillow. "Do you think my story will help others?" he asked.

I sat on a chair by his bed, transfixed by the potency of his words. "Yes, Ted," I managed to answer through my tight throat. "I think your story will help others."

At the time, I knew I'd witnessed a story of immense power and love, but years later, I can more clearly see its implication for all of us:

Love had strengthened his heart and spirit. Love had cast out his fear. The rose symbolized perfect love. He chose to receive the perfect love symbolized by the rose, and that was the secret behind his joy.

Ted's story reminds us we make choices as we face grief and loss. He chose to receive the love available through connection. He could have chosen to deny the love offered him. He could have chosen to remain isolated and bitter. But that's not the choice he made. He chose to receive love, and to quote him, "that made all the difference."

Ted told his story of connection with the hope it would help others find their way. When we follow his lead and dare to connect with love—to our beloved, to the world surrounding us, to the divine-within—then, like Ted, we will receive the ultimate consolation: the needed strength to endure our greatest grief, even as we die.

12

Obstacles

Ah! It is not the sea,
It is not the sea that sinks and shelves,
But ourselves
That rock and rise
With endless and uneasy motion,
Now touching the very skies,
Now sinking into the depths of ocean.

AH! IT IS NOT THE SEA, AS LONGFELLOW WRITES, but it's ourselves that "sink to the depths of the ocean." We rock and rise; we reach the skies; we sink to the depths. We choose, we act, and as Longfellow suggests, our obstacles to consolation are volitional and self-created.

One common obstacle to consolation is addiction.

In my social work practice, I've worked with clients who numbed grief's pain with drink or drugs. I've met men and women who'd binge-eat to avoid reality, or who refrained from eating to find a false sense of control. I've counseled ex-smokers who, in their grief, picked up a cigarette to smoke away their feelings. I've worked with clients who engaged in reckless sexual activity following the death of a loved one, and I've counseled those who hid from loneliness in rebound relationships.

But most often, I've met men and women who used compulsive work and over-scheduling to avoid grief, as illustrated by a group of scientists in a Fortune 500 company.

The human resources department had requested I meet with them following the death of a fellow employee. He was a young man, killed by a car while riding his bike during a charity event. His sudden death had shocked everyone.

We scheduled a meeting to address their concerns. More than fifty participants were expected to attend, but on the day of our session, only twelve showed up.

I wasn't surprised. Due to scheduling conflicts, it had been over a week since the young man's death. Many of his co-workers had attended his funeral a few days earlier, reducing the initial urgency for a grief session.

So I assumed the twelve in front of me knew him well and needed to further process their loss. But when this group of high-achieving scientists began to share their stories, I learned I was wrong.

Although respectful of the young man who had died and extremely sad about his early death, each member grieved an earlier loss. To my surprise, every one of them told a story about the un-mourned death of a parent, sibling, spouse, partner, or friend—*every one of them.*

The sudden death of their colleague awakened each of them to a previous loss, long buried beneath busy schedules and work demands. And now, as they sat around a table in a corporate conference room, they told their grief story for the first time. Then something happened.

They connected.

They connected to the memory of their beloved dead, and no longer feeling odd or alone, they connected to each other. As they connected, the numbness of un-mourned loss lifted, and deep sighs followed long-delayed tears.

Through the power of connection, the barrier to consolation, created by busy avoidance, had vanished.

We confront another obstacle to strength-giving consolation when we can't forgive ourselves and our loved ones for past hurts.

For years after Sue's death, I couldn't forgive my behavior on the morning of my wedding. I'd wanted all my bridesmaids to wear their hair up for the wedding processional. Although Sue wanted to wear her hair down, I refused. For years, I regretted my behavior.

Why, I later asked myself, did I insist on an upswept hairstyle when she felt prettier with her hair down? How could I cheat her of happiness when she had only months to live?

Guilt haunted me.

If only I wasn't a foolish, entitled bride; if only I'd listened to her; if only I could erase the past. My insistence on a hairstyle might seem like a minor infraction, but nothing is small that stabs at the heart.

My behavior shamed me. I tried to waken, in Longfellow's words, my "better soul that slumbers," but self-reproach had led to self-loathing, and my "better soul" seemed out of reach.

I knew I had to forgive myself, but I didn't know how until I recognized a fact I knew to be true:

Sue, from her better soul, would forgive me.

That realization helped me to connect to her love for me and receive her forgiveness. And through her love for me, I could finally gain access to my better soul and forgive myself.

Sue, through her love for me, taught me the importance of forgiveness, and that when our "better soul" meets the "better soul" of our beloved, we can forgive each other and ourselves. But when we don't forgive, we risk unnecessary anguish. When we don't forgive, we stay rooted in anger at ourselves and others. When we don't forgive, we block connection and deny ourselves consolation.

Fear is another major impediment to the strength-giving consolation we can receive through connection.

Several years ago, when psychiatrist Elizabeth Kubler-Ross, came to Philadelphia, she addressed the topic of fear. An audience of health care providers gathered at Temple University to hear her speak.

"How many of you," she asked in her Austrian accent, "have a fear of failure?"

Many in the audience raised their hands.

"How many have a fear of success?" she asked as hands again went up.

"Does anyone here," she finally asked, "have a fear of intimacy?"

She looked on the upraised arms and smiled. "None of these fears," she announced, "are natural fears."

A natural fear, she further explained, protects us from physical harm, such as falling from a high place. Irrational fear, she clarified, occurs when we're not in danger of bodily harm, yet the fear response is triggered. When fear—such as fear of failure, success, or intimacy—has been created in our minds, we're not in danger of bodily harm. "The danger is in your head," she told us. "It's not real. It's irrational."

But it can be difficult to differentiate instinctive, natural fears from our own created ones.

Our brains are hard-wired to be fearful. It's why the human species has survived. Our cavemen ancestors needed to listen for every breaking twig, as predators could pounce at any moment. Active fear made our ancestors fit to fight the battle of survival. Fear saved lives.

Today, we no longer live in constant danger of wild beasts attacking our fireside. Although our environment has changed, our brains haven't, and thanks to the laws of evolution, we're still naturally pre-disposed to life-saving rational fear. However, we can also be side-swiped by irrational fear.

Irrational fears penetrate our cultural beliefs about grief.

It's commonly feared that a continued relationship with our beloved indicates a pathological denial of death, but it's a misguided concept. Connection doesn't deny death. Unlike denial, connection supports us as we adjust to an environment without the physical presence of our loved one. Unlike denial, connection guides us to a new understanding about our relationship that doesn't end in death.

It's also commonly feared that continued relationships with the dead will sever relationships with the living, but connection counters this concern. Healthy connection leads to inclusion, not isolation. When love's energy flows through us, we fortify our bond with the human family and connect more strongly to others.

Sometimes, as we make new friends and begin new relationships, our loved ones harbor other fears. They fear we no longer remember the loved one who has died. Longfellow knew this, and before his second marriage, he sends an assuring letter to Mary's sister.

"Yes, my dear Eliza," he writes, "I am to be married again. My life was too lonely and restless—and I needed the soothing influences of a home; and I have chosen a person for my wife who possesses in a high degree those virtues and excellent traits of character which so distinguished my dear Mary. Think not, that in this new engagement, I do any wrong to her memory. I still retain, and ever shall preserve with sacred care all my cherished recollections of her truth, affection, and beautiful nature. And I feel that could she speak to me, she would approve of what I'm doing."

Just as Longfellow's connection to Mary didn't preclude a second marriage, connection with our beloved is *not* about closing our hearts to new relationships. Our heart has many chambers. Like Longfellow, we need not break old bonds to be able to love again.

Fear also shows its face when potential partners question our continued association with the deceased. Feeling threatened, they may overlook how lessons learned from the brevity of life can enrich new relationships. Eliza Potter, Mary's sister, and Fanny Appleton, Longfellow's second wife, offer an alternate choice.

Fanny, before her marriage to Longfellow, was concerned the Potter family would think poorly of her, and she dreaded any communication with them. That changed when Mary's sister Eliza removed her fears by writing a generous letter that approved Longfellow's choice for a second bride.

In return, Fanny sent Eliza a graceful reply that speaks warmly of Mary.

In her letter to Mary's sister, Fanny acknowledges her indebtedness to Longfellow's first wife. "His hope of a home," she writes, "—so sacred and dear to his loving nature" proceeded from his memories of Mary. "Blessed memories," Fanny adds, "to which I fervently pray to be found worthy to succeed."

From these women, we learn to open our hearts without fear. Like Eliza, family and friends can understand that new relationships don't erase the memory of loved ones from our hearts. Like Fanny, new life-partners can understand that our love for our departed beloved doesn't weaken our affection, but deepens it.

But for most of us, the greatest fear that blocks consolation is fear of death.

13

The Greatest Fear

"ALL FEAR IS ROOTED IN THE FEAR OF DEATH," writes poet and philosopher John O'Donohue.

To mitigate our fear, we hope for an after-life, but we live in a post-Darwinian age. We only believe what can be scientifically proven.

In the 1970s, a doctor published case studies that could suggest "life after death." In his book *Life After Life*, Raymond Moody documented similar experiences of people who regained consciousness after living through a clinical death.

As the spirit left the body, Moody reports, each of his subjects heard an uncomfortable noise. After moving through a dark tunnel, the spirits of dead family and friends would then greet them. Finally, Moody tells us, his subjects encountered a being of light—a warm and loving presence—that filled them with peace and joy.

However, in the intervening decades, new research has disputed the conclusion of "life after death."

Through the evolution of technology and neurology, scientists have been able to identify a physical process in the brain that occurs when the body is dying. They have learned that, when the brain shuts down, images displayed in the mind are identical to the tunnel and light imagery described in the life-after-death case studies.

So we now have the biological explanation for "out of body experiences" and "moving toward the light." For many, it's enough to stop believing again.

I might have stopped believing, too, if not for Mike, a hospital patient from my social work practice. Knowing him transfigured my own experience of death.

Mike had AIDS, and as his broken body dwindled towards death, I began to visit him daily. While I became one of his major supports, he became one of my most significant teachers. I think we both looked forward to our daily sessions.

One Friday afternoon, I walked into his room, but a strange, larger body lay in his bed.

"Where's Mike?" I panicked to myself while apologizing to the unknown patient for my intrusion into his room.

Eager to find him, I turned quickly on my heels, but I stopped in my tracks when the man in the bed called my name.

I moved slowly toward him. It *was* Mike.

Fluid retention had bloated his body beyond recognition. Knowing he didn't look like himself, he apologized for his altered appearance.

I tried not to look shocked at the changes in him as I approached his bedside.

Mike indicated the pillows propping his frail body. If he lay down, he told me, he would drown in the fluid that filled his lungs.

"It hurts to talk," he whispered.

"Then don't," I said.

I sat beside him. We held hands for a long time and said nothing until he broke the silence.

"When you come to work Monday, I won't be here," he said.

He didn't say, "I'm going to die." He didn't have to; I knew what he meant.

"Are you scared?" I asked.

Weary, he shook his head. "No. I just want to rest."

His eyes began to droop. I stayed beside him until he fell asleep. Subdued by sadness, I withdrew from his bedside and left his room.

Throughout the weekend, thoughts of Mike crossed my mind. While jogging through Rittenhouse Square on Saturday morning, I thought about him; while kneeling during Sunday's services at the old Jesuit Church, I thought about him.

Thoughts of Mike were embedded in my brain. It wouldn't have surprised me if they resurfaced in my dreams, in a Jungian-like release of the unconscious.

But nothing could have prepared me for what happened next.

Early Monday morning, something woke me from a deep sleep. I sat up with a jolt when I saw Mike standing at the foot of my bed.

I felt instructed to glance at the glow-lit numbers on my digital clock—it was 1:30 a.m.—and then to re-direct my attention to his face. He expressed nothing, verbally or emotionally, but he communicated a deep knowledge of serene being.

At the time, it didn't seem strange. Actually, it was very matter of fact. He didn't trouble or haunt me, but surrounded me with peace. I soon fell into a deep sleep.

On waking a few hours later, I wondered, "Was it a dream or a hallucination?"

Part of me hoped it was a dream; it would be more normal to dream than to hallucinate. Wanting to be normal, I concluded it was a dream. I decided that Mike couldn't have come to me after his death; that would be too bizarre. Plus—above all else—I hoped that he still lived.

After arriving at the hospital early Monday morning, I raced to the medical floor to check on Mike, but one thought gave me pause.

What if he isn't there?

My footsteps slowed. I couldn't face a bed without him in it. Instead, I slipped into the nurses' station to scan the log of patients who had died throughout the weekend.

My eyes skimmed the neatly penned list.

He didn't die Friday; he didn't die Saturday; he didn't die Sunday. My heart pounded against my chest. He isn't here! He isn't here! Then the back of my throat tightened when I saw what I didn't want to see. In black and white, pen on ledger, I read his name.

Blinking back tears, I forced myself to read the time of his death. I stared at the documented time and date: Monday, 1:30 a.m. The recorded time of his death matched the hour he had come to me.

Then I knew. *Mike had come to me in the night.*

It wasn't a dream, and it wasn't my imagination. Mike had come to me at the time of his death and imparted a truth long known by people of faith: At the time of death, the soul—the non-body life within us that houses the divine—departs the body and enters a state of being just beyond our own.

Mike was the first person to come to me after death, but he wasn't the only one.

After he died, other hospital patients also came to me after their death. But rather than seeing them as I saw Mike, I'd hear a whisper resonate in my ear. This audible sensation occurred frequently during my years on the oncology floor, and I would always know who had just died.

After hearing a whisper, I'd immediately look at my watch to note the time. On my return to the hospital, I'd then check the records kept at the nurses' station. Each time, the documented hour of death matched the time I'd observed.

It was always a patient at the hospital, with one exception: my friend Peter. I'd known Peter at Columbia. As grad students, we were head-residents in freshmen dorms, but after graduation, we'd lost touch.

Four years passed when, one early evening, recollections of Peter inhabited my mind. Everything I did was punctuated with a memory of my old friend.

"He'd kid me about this," I thought as I laid out my clothes for the following work-day, complete with scarf and matching shoes.

I remembered how he used to tease me. "You're such an Irish-American Princess," he'd kid in a warm tone, amusement in his eyes.

Throughout the night and the following morning, I thought about Peter. I recalled how he'd often arrive at my door with a whimsical gift, like a red crisp leaf in autumn or the first snowball in December. I remembered how he'd escort me to school dances, and how our freshmen women would fantasize we were married.

Peter—tall, blonde, and charming—loved to indulge them. With a conspiratorial wink at me, he'd flash them his winning smile as he draped a casual arm around my shoulder. In response, they'd practically swoon as they gave my handsome escort an approving nod followed by a sigh.

With a sudden urgency, I wanted to call him, but I had no way to reach him. In that deep-beneath place, I felt a hollow ache. I missed him.

Then I felt the familiar whisper in my ear.

Instinctively, I looked at my watch. I was puzzled. None of my patients were dying. Then my heart turned over.

"Peter!" I thought.

That afternoon, I received a telephone call from the assistant dean of students at Columbia. Peter and I had worked with her during our years as head residents in the student dorms.

"I thought you'd want to know," she kindly told me, "that Peter died this morning."

Somehow I managed to thank her. Then I hung up the phone, crumbled to the floor, and buried my face in my knees.

No! Not Peter!

I instinctively denied it. Morning, noon and night, he'd been with me in joyful reminiscence. He'd inserted himself so vividly in my mind, I almost expected him at my front door.

It can't be.

But denial couldn't long refute what I already knew. That same chilling whisper that had announced so many deaths had foretold the sad news. I sat immobile on the floor and cried for hours.

Then insight stunned me with awareness:

Peter had come to me, as Mike had done years earlier, to say "goodbye."

Like Mike, his essence—made known through the memories and the soft audible sensation—had transcended the limitations of his body. Peter's life in clay form had ended, but not his life in the spirit.

Acknowledging his presence soothed my anguish; connecting with him gave me deep-beneath peace and strength; and amid this great mystery of life and death, I received the grace of consolation.

It wouldn't have been possible without Mike. Mike had first invited me to witness the liberation of the spirit from the confinement of the body. Mike had sensitized me to recognize the presence of Peter and other patients as they died.

Mike not only transfigured my own fear of death, but by influencing my work at the hospital, he helped to transfigure the fear of others.

"I just want to rest," Mike had told me before he died. One year later, his words guided me as I sat by the bedside of Joe, another young man dying from AIDS.

The virus had ravaged Joe's body. With sightless eyes open, he lay on his bed in a hepatic coma, his breathing deep and steady.

Taking his hand, I spoke in the most soothing tone I could manage.

"You're in a safe place, Joe. You're in the hospital, and everyone here wants to help you."

Remembering Mike's words before he died, I added, "You just breathe and rest."

The power of the words filled me with foreboding. Wasn't I giving him permission to die? I wanted life for Joe, not death, but I also wanted him to find comfort.

I swallowed hard and repeated the words Mike had spoken a year earlier. "Today is a good day to rest, Joe," I said. "Today, you can rest."

In the doorway, a cluster of nurses gathered to watch me. To them, it seemed idiotic to speak to a patient in a coma. Elbowing each other, they talked behind hands that didn't hide their ridicule. One of them marched into the room, knuckles fisted on her hips.

"You don't really think he can hear you?" she scorned.

Before I could respond, Joe sat up in bed. The young nurse froze.

With focused urgency, he directed his gaze at me. He then took a deep, laboring breath and exhaled the ancient sound, "OM."

Joe was an African-American, bible-reading Baptist. He didn't, to my knowledge, practice yoga or follow Hindu teachings. Yet his last words were "OM," Hinduism's most sacred word. According to Hindu teaching, "OM" represents the divine that permeates our life through our breath. The sound of the voiced "OM" also corresponds to the act of creation.

Without vibration—according to Hindu belief—there would be no creation. Vibration set creation in motion; the same vibration is released when the word "OM" is vocalized. In the Hindu faith, "OM" is the hum of new life and releases a pulsing energy similar to the original vibration that caused creation.

In a juxtaposition of opposites, Joe chanted "OM," the Hindu sound of creation and birth, as he lay dying.

With his hand in mine, I could feel the vibration of his voice surge through my body with a jolt of energy that, like a power line, connected me to him.

A silent pause followed his first intonation.

Stupefied, the nurse's arms dropped to her side. "He's speaking to you," she gasped.

As though in response, Joe inhaled deeply and lengthened his torso. On the exhale of his breath, he proclaimed a stronger, more resonant "OM."

In the pause between his pronouncements, a long, sad sob sounded from the hall and pierced the silence.

For an instant, I looked away from Joe and toward the doorway where I saw his mother, in a spasm of grief, bolstered by two nurses.

"Oh! My only child!" she keened. "Oh! Don't you leave me!"

While the nurses provided her comfort, my focus returned to Joe. I watched him respond to her sorrow.

With a sharp inhale of oxygen, his spine strained to further lengthen his upright torso. On the exhale, he directed his last, urgent "OM" to his mother as she collapsed onto the floor. Then his head fell back upon the pillows, his arms limp on the bed.

In the stillness that followed, his nurse and I stayed by Joe's bed, unable to move.

"Strange as it may sound," writes philosopher O'Donohue,

"we will come to trust death as the deeper dignity within us carries us through the travail of departure."

All in the room witnessed what O'Donohue had described: At the moment of death, the deeper dignity within Joe had carried him across the threshold. Through the power of the eternal "OM," the infinite within him became manifest. Through the power of the holy word, his death became his second birth.

At the moment of his death, a sacred presence overshadowed the room and gifted all who were present, including Joe's mother, with a deep-beneath grace.

"I am so grateful I was there," his mother later told me. "I saw my son at rest. I saw him at peace."

"At death," writes O'Donohue, "the infinite within us will come good: there is no need to be afraid."

My father, in his last hours, had no fear. He couldn't wait to see his mother, son, and daughter who had died before him. He longed to join them, embraced by God in love.

In his last moments, connection sustained him.

He'd cultivated the habit of connection as a boy. His mother had died when he was two, but throughout his life, he'd felt her unseen presence. From his mother, he had learned to reach into the space between them, to receive her love, and to give it in return. His mother had taught him that relationships don't end in death, and through her, he'd experienced the power of consolation only received through connection.

Years later, when his baby daughter died and he visited her little grave every morning, he could feel his mother's love surround him as he wept and prayed. In that dark hour, his habit of connection—developed since childhood—supported him with the knowledge that his baby girl was not alone, but with God and with his mother.

Consolation, a gift first realized through his lifelong connection to his mother, also graced him as he lay dying.

"Don't feel sorry for me," he reassured all who gathered by his bedside. "I'm going *home*."

All his life, he'd experienced infinite love through connection—to his beloved dead, to the world surrounding him, and to the divine-within. A lifetime of connection had prepared him for his hour of death.

From his hospital bed, he welcomed the presence of his beloved dead—and the divine love surrounding all of them—with utter joy. The infinite love within him "came good," as O'Donohue teaches, and brought my father, as he lay dying, to a soul-dwelling peace.

This soul-dwelling peace, which is consolation itself, is realized through the power of connection. It removes anxiety and transfigures our greatest fear—fear of death—even as we die.

We need only to connect to the sacred space of love between us and our beloved; to the sacred space of love between us and the world that surrounds us; and to the sacred space of love between us and the divine-within.

Only connect, and consolation will grace us—through life *and* death—with fear-conquering peace.

14

The Wisdom of Grief

GRIEF CAN BE A HOLY TIME LEADING TO contemplation and spiritual formation. It invites us to slow down and make deliberate life choices.

Grief helps us discover how the smallest details linger in the heart's memory: the sound of a loved one's voice on the phone, the small breath of a sleeping child in our arms, the colors in the sky at sunset, the convivial sharing of food with friends. Through grief, we learn that nothing is too minor to celebrate or too insignificant to enjoy.

When we know that we don't have "forever," we learn to express love now. We live the gift that is today, so that tomorrow there will be no regrets. This makes life holy and sacred—to see the love that surrounds us, to receive it, and to act on it.

When we recognize the worth in all that surrounds us—the seen and the unseen—we uncover the essence of life. "What is essential," Antoine de Saint-Exupery writes in *The Little Prince*, "is invisible to the eye."

Wonder is our gateway to the invisible, and grief compels us to seek it.

When seen through the lens of grief, the ordinary can become extraordinary: the sunrise, a newborn puppy, a baby's first steps, a starlit sky. By teaching us not to take life for granted, grief helps us to cultivate a new way of perceiving the world around us. Only then can we experience wonder—life's daily miracles—and see the essential that's invisible to the eye.

Grief brings other insights. Years ago, I walked Dublin's city streets beside a friend who, like me, spent his junior year at Ireland's Trinity College. As we crossed O'Connell Street, he said something that seemed wise beyond his twenty years.

"Why can't everyone be good to each other?" he asked. "We're all just going to die, anyway. Why not be good to each other until then?"

Perhaps grief had taught him to perceive the human race with acute sensitivity, as it can change how we view our fractious, competitive world. Grief teaches us compassion, which means "to suffer with." Only by suffering our own grief can we begin to understand the suffering of others. By joining them in their pain, we can then become an instrument of compassion for those who mourn.

Compassionate expression of grief is best communicated through love. The play *Steel Magnolias,* written by a brother grieving the death of his sister, reflects his love for her; Longfellow's "Footsteps of Angels" honors the beloved memory of his young wife; my brother, as he parents his children, reflects his love for their mother.

Grief has as many expressions and forms as there are people who have loved and lost. But for all who have lost, the love remains.

When our love, which is interior and invisible to the eye, finds an external form, it makes love visible. Through this outer expression of our love—such as a painting, book, poem, or play—others who are bereaved can see their own love reflected. By helping them to connect to the love surrounding them, our "love made visible" becomes a source of consolation to others.

The roots are love, it leads to love, and it inspires love. It begins with our love for one person and their love for us. Our love for each other, stronger than death, eternally connects us. Our expression of that relationship, rooted in love, can give solace to those who long to connect with their own loved ones but don't know how. This love between us and our beloved, released to the universe, can now be received by those who need it. So love begets the work of love, comforting those who have loved and lost in a never-ending continuum of consolation.

It leads us to a new understanding: The nucleus of grief is love. Without love, there is no grief. We only grieve what we've loved and lost.

But the love never goes away.

In the throes of deep sorrow, the pain is felt but not the love. Through connection, love reclaims its place in our hearts. Love lasts.

For all who grieve, connection—to our beloved, to the love in the world, and to the divine-within—is our labor of love.

In Longfellow's *Evangeline*, the Abbot gives wise counsel:

Talk not of wasted affection, affection never was wasted;
If it enrich not the heart of another, its waters, returning
Back to their springs, like the rain, shall fill them full of refreshment;
That which the fountain sends forth returns again to the fountain.
Patience; accomplish thy labor;
Accomplish thy work of affection!
Sorrow and silence are strong, and patient endurance is godlike,
Therefore accomplish thy labor of love till the heart is made godlike,
Purified, strengthened, perfected, and rendered more worthy of heaven.

"Accomplish thy work of affection," writes Longfellow. For all who grieve, connection is our work of affection; connection is our labor of love. When we connect, then consolation—like water returning to the fountain—replenishes our strength.

But there will still be days when consolation eludes us. Days when we cry for help; days when, despite efforts to connect, we feel empty; days when we're desperate for the consolation that follows connection but receive nothing.

What then?

During times of despair when God seems absent, it helps to remember that divine love waits for us. Sometimes we have to listen carefully for the still, small voice that heals.

On December 26, 2004, tidal waves destroyed villages in fourteen countries in South Asia. The quaking earth and flooding waters wiped out tribes and killed thousands of men, women, and children.

In the aftermath of the tsunami, religious leaders worldwide were asked, "Why did this happen? Why would God do this terrible thing to innocent people?"

Responding from London, Jonathan Sacks, Chief Rabbi of the United Hebrew Congregation of the Commonwealth, writes that God placed us in a physical world, and physical disasters happen within its parameters. Blizzards, hurricanes, tornadoes, mudslides, electrical storms, and earthquakes batter and slice the earth, and—yes—innocents die in their wake.

Then he reminds us what God taught Elijah: God is not in the earthquake, or the whirlwind that destroys but "in the still, small voice that heals."

In other words, God—or Love—is in the connection, the sacred "space between us" that follows heartbreak. No matter how seeming small the voice, it graces us with God's care as it answers our heart.

"We carry within us a deep strain of God's caring," writes John O'Donohue. "Anywhere care comes alive, God is present."

This infinite love, this "deep strain of God's caring," is between us, around us, and within us. It's denied to no one, regardless of age, sex, nationality, ethnicity, race, or religion.

This "still, small voice that heals"—this infinite love—is made manifest to all through connection.

We need only to connect. Connection *and* living the question, "what does life, at this moment, ask of me," leads us to give love, receive love, and live the life we were put on this planet to live. Without fail, it opens the heart to consolation's benediction.

For me, it led to a homecoming for the soul.

* * *

Before Sue's death, I had prayed the prayer we all pray when someone we love is dying. I'd never prayed with more intensity than when I knelt by her side and opened my heart with vulnerability I had never before known.

"Please God, don't make us lose her," I begged.

Two weeks later, Sue called with news that her doctor could find no signs of cancer on the x-ray.

I was elated. Not only had my prayer been answered, but it was the answer I wanted. God would keep her with us.

To me, this answer to prayer verified that God listened, responded, and actually cared. Such direct knowledge lifted all burdens and made my sense of being so light that nothing could weigh me down. But the exhilaration didn't last. We soon learned that the x-ray was wrong, and a few weeks later, Sue was dead.

I felt betrayed. What kind of taunting God would offer hope only to withdraw it? I responded to God's seeming indifference with anger, followed by years of deliberate avoidance.

As time moved on, my spiritual exile began to bother me. I needed closure. I had questions to ask and a score to settle. It was time to confront the Divine that had denied me.

With Sue's purse swinging by my side, I made my way to Portland's majestic cathedral and scaled the flight of concrete steps beneath the church spires. I pulled on the polished oak door but paused in the entrance.

It had been years since I'd trusted the peace within these walls.

With tentative steps, I crossed the marble tiles and slid into an empty pew. Surrounded by silence, I addressed God in all my desolation.

Why did you take Sue away? Why did you promise—in the depths of my prayer—to keep her with me?

"God is in the still, small voice that heals," Rabbi Sacks teaches us, but I heard only silence.

Then I touched the leather purse on my lap.

An immediate connection to Sue stopped the chattering chaos within me. Stillness followed as a sense of knowing entered that deep-beneath-me place.

Sue had been—and always will—be with me.

The promise had been kept.

Like Elijah before me, I fell to my knees, and for the first time in years, I bowed my head and began to pray.

* * *

Afterword

IT'S BEEN MANY YEARS SINCE SUE DIED, ALTHOUGH it seems like yesterday. I follow Longfellow's example for living with grief, and in blessed memory, I keep her with me every day.

I live in Portland, Longfellow's native town, and on this early morning in Maine, I look to the same horizon he once did. In the aftermath of a January blizzard, Casco Bay is a silver sheet shimmering in the light of the rising sun.

As the white blaze illuminates the dawn, I think how Longfellow lived a life fully connected despite a life filled with loss. In the deepest winter of his years, he truly understood how the strength-giving form of love—received through connection to the beloved, to the world, and to the divine-within—brings consolation.

It's our beacon of light in the darkest depths of grief.

Nine days before he died, Longfellow left his sickbed to add these last words to the last lines of his last poem, in one last message of consolation for all of us:

> Out of the shadows of night
> The world rolls into light;
> It is daybreak everywhere.

I look to the sunrise, and out of the shadows of night, I see what Longfellow sees: Light is there. It is always there. It is everywhere.

* * *

Acknowledgments

I AM INDEBTED TO THE PATIENTS AND FAMILIES at Memorial Sloan Kettering and Lankenau Hospitals who taught me, through life example, about the power of connection, and to the Maine Historical Society for introducing me to Longfellow. I am extremely grateful to both groups of benefactors for transforming my grief and making this book possible.

I'm grateful to all who've helped form *Voices of the Night*. It began as a letter to a young widow, and I send a special acknowledgment to Kristin and to the Larkin family who continue to live with the grief that never, entirely, heals. My personal letter to Kristin expanded to a book that has matured through many versions and reflects feedback from many readers. For this final version, I'm beholden to all of you.

During many years of writing, I've been blessed by friends and family who've sustained me and encouraged me in this project. I could not have completed *Voices of the Night* without your support. I'm also grateful to those whose stories are included in these pages. You all continue to inspire me.

Thank you also to Grace Peirce, my extraordinary book shepherd. Your sensitivity to the subject, passion for the written word, smart edits and keen book design transformed *Voices of the Night* from a word document manuscript to an award-winning book, an honor I gratefully share with you.

I send a special thank you to my brother, John J. Kallaugher, and to his children, John and Alice, for allowing me to share our grief story; to my extraordinary mother, Barbara Kallaugher, who continues to model grace, love, and courage while living with grief; to my friend, Ann Walker, who encouraged my honest disclosure and left our world too soon; to Jeff Berman,

Professor of English at the University of Albany, whose book *Risky Writing* dared me to bare my grief rather than conceal it with intellectual distance; to Ken Happe of blessed memory, my remarkable mentor and teacher, who taught me to risk and begin; and to Anthony Kuzniewski, S.J., for inspiring me to seek heroes in history.

This book would not have been possible without the support of Steve Cannon, my husband and soul mate. I am forever grateful for his guidance, love, and care. I'm also indebted to our beautiful daughter Rose for bringing love and meaning to our lives and whose patience through hours of research and writing has gifted me with this work of generativity. Finally, I would not have written *Voices of the Night* without the influence of my sister, Evelyn Kallaugher, who first taught me that relationships don't end in death.

I close with a message of profound thanks to my father, John M. Kallaugher. On our last morning together, he urged me to finish this book and share it with others. So now, graced by Consolation received through his connection to me, I present *Voices of the Night* with gratitude and love.

— Appendix —

A PSALM OF LIFE
And Other Consolation Poems

Nineteenth-Century Guidelines for Twenty-First-Century Readers

THESE POEMS HAVE GIVEN STRENGTH TO men and women for over a century, and they can give us strength, too.

Sam Ward, Longfellow's friend, received a copy of *Voices of the Night* following the death of his father.

"I have not yet thanked you," he writes the poet, "for the exquisite messengers. They have stolen to my heart in many a night of sorrow and mitigated the bitterness of despair."

Like Longfellow's friend, all of us can receive the gift of consolation offered in these poems, even if we're not accustomed to metered poetry. It's easy when we follow the guidelines of nineteenth-century readers.

First, according to poet-artist Washington Allston, we must be in the mood to read the poems. It's important for the reader—as well as the writer—to be in a receptive frame of mind.

Second, it's helpful to not only read the poems once but to re-read them, like author Nathaniel Hawthorne and his approach to metered rhyme.

"I read your poems," Hawthorne writes Longfellow, "over and over and over again, and continue to read them at all my leisure hours; and they grow upon me at every re-perusal."

The final recommendation is to not speed-read through

these poems but to approach them as we would prayer or meditation. When we take the time to read a poem, it can soothe our restless hearts, much like "the benediction," writes Longfellow, "that follows after prayer."

So let us select a poem. Then, after calming our inner-most self, let us read and re-read it. After we repeat it and make it our own, let us ponder it, like a prayer. When we do, the poem will steal to our hearts. It will connect us to the poet and to all who have preceded us. It will connect us to our departed beloved and to the divine-within. Through this connection, in a powerful sweep of consolation, it will mitigate the bitterness of despair.

Like Sam Ward, may all of us find consolation in these pages; may all of us know we are not alone in our sorrow; and may all of us receive—through the power of connection—strength and peace.

A PSALM OF LIFE

(WHAT THE HEART OF THE YOUNG MAN SAID TO THE PSALMIST)

Included in his first published volume of poetry, Voices of the Night, *Longfellow said of this poem: "I kept it sometime in manuscript, unwilling to show it to any one, it being a voice from my inmost heart, at a time when I was rallying from depression." The psalmist in the poem, Longfellow later explained, is the poet himself.*

According to Longfellow's brother, the "Psalm of Life" roused many to "high resolve, and wakened them to a new sense of meaning and worth of life." Longfellow re-iterates the psalm's core principle in his reply to a teacher after receiving birthday cards from the class. In his letter, Longfellow encourages the students to live their own psalm of life. He writes, "I can only send my greeting to the grand army of your pupils, and ask you to tell them, as I am sure you told them before, to live up to the best that is in them; to live noble lives."

Tell me not, in mournful numbers,
Life is but an empty dream!
For the soul is dead that slumbers,
And things are not as they seem.

Life is real! Life is earnest!
And the grave is not its goal;
Dust thou art, to dust returnest,
Was not spoken of the soul.

Not enjoyment and not sorrow,
Is our destined end or way;
But to act, that each to-morrow
Find us farther than to-day.

Art is long and time is fleeting,
And our hearts, though stout and brave,
Still, like muffled drums, are beating
Funeral marches to the grave.

In the world's broad field of battle,
In the bivouac of Life,
Be not like dumb, driven cattle!
Be a hero in the strife!

Trust no future, howe'er pleasant!
Let the dead Past bury its dead!
Act, – act in the living Present!
Heart within, and God o'erhead!

Lives of great men all remind us
We can make our lives sublime,
And, departing, leave behind us
Footprints on the sands of time;

Footprints, that perhaps another,
Sailing o'er life's solemn main,
A forlorn and shipwrecked brother,
Seeing, shall take heart again.

Let us, then, be up and doing,
With a heart for any fate;
Still achieving, still pursuing,
Learn to labor and to wait.

THE LIGHT OF STARS

"This poem was written on a beautiful summer night. The moon, a little strip of silver, was just setting behind the groves of Mount Auburn [where Mary Longfellow was buried], and the planet Mars blazing in the southeast. There was a singular light in the sky." H.W.L.

The night is come, but not too soon;
And sinking silently,
All silently, the little moon
Drops down behind the sky.

There is no light in earth or heaven
But the cold light of stars;
And the first watch of night is given
To the red planet Mars.

Is it the tender star of love?
The star of love and dreams?
Oh no! from that blue tent above
A hero's armor gleams.

And earnest thoughts within me rise,
When I behold afar,
Suspended in the evening skies,
The shield of that red star.

O star of strength! I see thee stand
And smile upon my pain;
Thou beckonest with thy mailed hand
And I am strong again.

Within my breast there is no light
But the cold light of stars;
I give the first watch of the night
To the red planet Mars.

The star of the unconquered will,
He rises in my breast,
Serene, and resolute, and still,
And calm, and self-possessed.

And thou, too, whosoe'er thou art,
That readest this brief psalm,
As one by one thy hopes depart,
Be resolute and calm.

Oh, fear not in a world like this,
And thou shalt know erelong,
Know how sublime a thing it is
To suffer and be strong.

HYMN TO THE NIGHT

"The setting of a great hope is like the setting of the sun," writes Longfellow. "The brightness of our life is gone. Shadows of evening fall around us, and the world seems but a dim reflection, – itself a broader shadow. We look forward into the coming lonely night. The soul withdraws into itself. Then stars arise, and the night is holy." H.W.L.

I heard the trailing garments of the Night
Sweep through her marble halls!
I saw her sable skirts all fringed with light
From the celestial walls!

I felt her presence, by its spell of might,
Stoop o'er me from above;
The calm, majestic presence of the Night,
As of the one I love.

I heard the sounds of sorrow and delight,
The manifold, soft chimes,
That fill the haunted chambers of the Night,
Like some old poet's rhymes.

From the cool cisterns of the midnight air
My spirit drank repose;
The fountain of perpetual peace flows there, –
From those deep cisterns flows.

O holy Night! From thee I learn to bear
What man has borne before!
Thou layest thy finger on the lips of Care,
And they complain no more.

Peace! Peace! Orestes-like I breathe this prayer!
Descend with broad-winged flight,
The welcome, the thrice-prayed for, the most fair,
The best-beloved Night!

THE RAINY DAY

In the years following Mary's death, Longfellow fought depressive thoughts and ill health; Fanny Appleton's initial refusal to marry him only reinforced his despondency. In an earlier journal entry, he writes: "A dismal, rainy day. Sorrow seeks out such days as these." While visiting his family's home in Portland, Maine, he writes the following poem during a rainstorm.

The day is cold, and dark, and dreary;
It rains, and the wind is never weary;
The vine still clings to the mouldering wall
But at every gust the dead leaves fall,
And the day is dark and dreary.

My life is cold and dark and dreary;
It rains, and the wind is never weary;
My thoughts still cling to the mouldering Past,
But the hopes of youth fall thick in the blast,
And the days are dark and dreary.

Be still, sad heart! and cease repining;
Behind the clouds is the sun still shining;
Thy fate is the common fate of all,
Into each life some rain must fall,
Some days must be dark and dreary.

MEZZO CAMMIN

Written at Boppard on the Rhine, August 25, 1842, just before leaving for home.

Annie Fields, friend and wife of Longfellow's publisher, remembers how he suffered with grief and unrequited love. "In 1842," she writes, "he again visited Europe, for the third time. His health suffered from solitude and the continued activities of the mind. 'I sometimes think,' he said, 'that no one with a head and a heart can be perfectly well.' Therefore in the spring, he went abroad to try the water cure at Marienberg.... His mind was full of poems. He wrote one sonnet called 'Mezzo Cammin,' never printed until after his death; perhaps he thought it too expressive of personal sadness."

Half of my life is gone, and I have let
The years slip from me and have not fulfilled
The aspiration of my youth, to build
Some tower of song with lofty parapet.
Not indolence, nor pleasure, nor the fret
Of restless passions that would not be stilled,
But sorrow, and a care that almost killed,
Kept me from what I may accomplish yet;
Though, half-way up the hill, I see the Past
Lying beneath me with its sounds and sights, –
A city in the twilight dim and vast,
With smoking roofs, soft bells, and gleaming lights, –
And hear above me on the autumnal blast
The cataract of Death far thundering from the heights.

THE BRIDGE

Longfellow's fortunes change when Fanny Appleton accepts his proposal of marriage. "Life was too lonely—and sad," he writes his sister, "with little to soothe and calm me. Now the Future opens its long closed gates into pleasant fields and lands of quiet. The strife and struggle are over, for a season, at least; and the troubled spirit findeth its perfect rest." For a season, at least, he enjoys domestic harmony and raises five children with his beloved second wife while remembering an earlier time when sorrow filled his heart.

I stood on the bridge at midnight,
As the clocks were striking the hour,
And the moon rose o'er the city,
Behind the dark church-tower.

I saw her bright reflection
In the waters under me,
Like a golden goblet falling
And sinking into the sea.

And far in the hazy distance
Of that lovely night in June,
The blaze of the flaming furnace
Gleamed redder than the moon.

Among the long, black rafters
The wavering shadows lay,
And the current that came from the ocean
Seemed to lift and bear them away;

As, sweeping and eddying through them,
Rose the belated tide,
And, streaming into the moonlight,
The seaweed floated wide.

And like those waters rushing
Among the wooden piers,
A flood of thoughts came o'er me
That filled my eyes with tears.

How often, oh how often,
In the days that had gone by,
I had stood on that bridge at midnight
And gazed on that wave and sky!

How often, oh, how often,
I had wished that ebbing tide
Would bear me away on its bosom
O'er the ocean wild and wide!

For my heart was hot and restless,
And my life was full of care,
And the burden laid upon me
Seemed greater than I could bear.

But now it has fallen from me,
It is buried in the sea;
And only the sorrow of others
Throws its shadow over me.

Yet whenever I cross the river
On its bridge with wooden piers,
Like the odor of brine from the ocean
Comes the thought of other years.

And I think how many thousands
Of care-encumbered men,
Each bearing his burden of sorrow,
Have crossed the bridge since then.

I see the long procession
Still passing to and fro,
The young heart hot and restless,
And the old subdued and slow!

And forever and forever,
As long as the river flows,
As long as the heart has passions,
As long as life has woes;

The moon and its broken reflection
And its shadows shall appear,
As the symbol of love in heaven,
And its wavering image here.

RESIGNATION

Longfellow's journal entries reflect a happy family life. During one idyllic summer, day-time adventures included frolics with the children. "We all took a stroll to the lake," he writes, "The children paddled about, barefooted, in the water; and we pushed off in a flat-bottomed boat, half-full of water, in pursuit of water lilies. Then we had lunch on the pebbly shore."

The Longfellow family would have never predicted the sorrow they'd soon face. A month later, the youngest lay "patient and mournful, overcome by the heat." After three days, she seemed to improve. "When a child is ill in a house," Longfellow records, "all the usual course of things is interrupted. All thoughts centre in the little patient. Ours is better to-day."

But their hopes for her recovery weren't realized, and ten days later, she died. For a long time, Longfellow sat alone beside her. He writes in his journal: "The twilight fell softly on her placid face and the white flowers she held in her little hands. In the deep silence, the bird sang from the hall, a sad strain, a melancholy requiem. It touched and soothed me." Two months later, he adds the following entry: "I feel very sad today. I miss very much my dear little Fanny. An unappeasable longing to see her comes over me at times, which I can hardly control." Shortly afterward, he writes a requiem of his own for the daughter who died too soon.

There is no flock, however watched and tended,
But one dead lamb is there!
There is no fireside, howsoe-er defended,
But has one vacant chair!

The air is full of farewells to the dying,
And mournings for the dead;
The heart of Rachel, for her children crying,
Will not be comforted!

Let us be patient! These severe afflictions
Not from the ground arise,
But oftentimes celestial benedictions
Assume this dark disguise.

We see but dimly through the mists and vapors;
Amid these earthly damps
What seems to us but sad, funereal tapers
May be heaven's distant lamps.

There is no Death! What seems so is transition;
This life of mortal breath
Is but a suburb of the life elysian,
Whose portal we call Death.

She is not dead, – the child of our affection, –
But gone into that school
Where she no longer needs our poor protection,
And Christ himself doth rule.

In that great cloister's stillness and seclusion,
By guardian angels led,
Safe from temptation, safe from sin's pollution,
She lives, whom we call dead.

Day after day we think what she is doing
In those bright realms of air;
Year after year, her tender steps pursuing,
Behold her grown more fair.

Thus do we walk with her, and keep unbroken
The bond which nature gives,
Thinking that our remembrance, though unspoken,
May reach her where she lives.

Not as a child shall we again behold her;
For when with raptures wild
In our embraces we again enfold her,
She will not be a child;

But a fair maiden, in her Father's mansion,
Clothed with celestial grace;
And beautiful with all the soul's expansion
Shall we behold her face.

And though at times impetuous with emotion
And anguish long suppressed,
The swelling heart heaves moaning like the ocean,
That cannot be at rest, –

We will be patient, and assuage the feeling
We may not wholly stay;
By silence sanctifying, not concealing,
The grief that must have way.

THE CROSS OF SNOW

Longfellow experienced more personal tragedy when his wife Fanny, while melting sealing wax to preserve locks of her daughters' hair in an envelope, caught fire from a stray match. With flames engulfing her, she came to him. He tried to save her. He wrapped her in blankets and used his hands to keep the fire from her face, but she died the next morning.

"Three days later," writes Samuel Longfellow, the poet's brother and biographer, "her burial took place at Mount Auburn. It was the anniversary of her marriage-day; and on her beautiful head, lovely and unmarred in death; some hand had placed a wreath of orange blossoms. Her husband was not there,—confined to his chamber by the severe burns which he had himself received."

After Fanny's death, Longfellow raised their five children, noting in his journal on Christmas day: "How inexpressibly sad are all holidays! But the dear little girls had their Christmas-tree last night; and an unseen presence blessed the scene."

According to Longfellow's brother, "He bore his grief with courage and in silence. Only after months had passed could he speak of it; and then only in fewest words. To a brother far distant he wrote: 'And now, of what we both are thinking I can write no word. God's will be done.' To a visitor, who expressed the hope that he might be enabled to 'bear his cross' with patience, he replied: 'BEAR the cross, yes; but what if one is stretched upon it!'"

Longfellow wrote this sonnet eighteen years after the death of Fanny. It was found in his desk drawer after he died.

THE CROSS OF SNOW

In the long, sleepless watches of the night,
A gentle face – the face of one long dead –
Looks at me from the wall, where round its head
The night-lamp casts a halo of pale light.
Here in this room she died; and soul more white
Never through martyrdom of fire was led
To its repose; nor can in books be read
The legend of a life more benedight.
There is a mountain in the distant West
That, sun-defying, in its deep ravines
Displays a cross of snow upon its side.
Such is the cross I wear upon my breast
These eighteen years, through all the changing scenes
And seasons, changeless since the day she died.

THREE FRIENDS OF MINE

Following multiple losses, Longfellow writes a series of five sonnets commemorating three friends.

In stanza II, Longfellow honors Cornelius Felton, his first friend at Cambridge. A professor of Greek at Harvard College, Felton served as its president before his sudden death at age fifty-five.

In stanza III, he laments the loss of Louis Agassiz, another renowned Harvard teacher and one of the great scientists of his day.

In stanza IV, he commemorates Charles Sumner, the senator from Massachusetts from 1851-1874, who was a major force in the fight against slavery. Longfellow calls these sonnets, in a letter to a friend, "my small tribute to their memory."

I

When I remember them, those friends of mine,
Who are no longer there, the noble three,
Who half my life were more than friends to me,
And whose discourse was like a generous wine.
I most remember the divine
Something that shone in them, and made us see
The archetypal man, and what might be
The amplitude of nature's first design.
In vain I stretch my hands to clasp their hands;
I cannot find them. Nothing now is left
But a majestic memory. They meanwhile
Wander together in Elysian lands,
Perchance remembering me, who am bereft
Of their dear presence, and, remembering, smile.

II

Attica thy birthplace should have been,
Or the Ionian Isles, or where the seas
Encircle in their arms the Cyclades,
So wholly Greek wast thou in thy serene

And childlike joy of life, O Philhellene!
Around thee would have swarmed the Attic bees;
Homer had been thy friend, or Socrates,
And Plato welcomed thee to his demesne.
For thee old legends breathed historic breath;
Thou sawest Poseidon in the purple sea,
And in the sunset Jason's fleece of gold!
O, what hadst thou to do with cruel Death,
Who wast so full of life, or Death with thee,
That thou shouldst die before thou hadst grown old!

III

I stand again on the familiar shore,
And hear the waves of the distracted sea
Piteously calling and lamenting thee,
And waiting restless at thy cottage door.
The rocks, the sea-weed on the ocean floor,
The willows in the meadow, and the free
Wild winds of the Atlantic welcome me;
Then why shouldst thou be dead, and come no more?
Ah, why shouldst thou be dead, when common men
Are busy with their trivial affairs,
Having and holding? Why, when thou hadst read
Nature's mysterious manuscript, and then
Wast ready to reveal the truth it bears,
Why art thou silent? Why shouldst thou be dead?

IV

River, that stealest with such silent pace
Around the City of the Dead, where lies
A friend who bore thy name, and whom these eyes
Shall see no more in his accustomed place,
Linger and fold him in thy soft embrace
And say good night, for now the western skies
Are red with sunset, and gray mists arise

Like damps that gather on a dead man's face.
Good night! Good night! as we have so oft said
Beneath this roof at midnight in the days
That are no more, and shall no more return.
Thou hast but taken thy lamp and gone to bed;
I stay a little longer, as one stays
To cover up the embers that still burn.

V

The doors are all wide open; at the gate
The blossomed lilacs counterfeit a blaze,
And seem to warm the air; a dreamy haze
Hangs o'er the Brighton meadows like a fate,
And on their margin, with sea-tides elate,
The flooded Charles, as in the happier days,
Writes the last letter of his name, and stays
His restless steps, as if compelled to wait.
I also wait; but they will come no more,
Those friends of mine, whose presence satisfied
The thirst and hunger of my heart. Ah me!
They have forgotten the pathway to my door!
Something is gone from nature since they died,
And summer is not summer, nor can be.

AUF WIEDERSEHEN

In Memory of J.T.F.

On April 29, 1881, Longfellow writes in his journal: "A sorrowful and distracted week. Fields died on Sunday, the 24th. Palfrey died on Tuesday. Two intimate friends in one week!" In response to his loss, Longfellow dedicates the following poem to the memory of his publisher and friend, James Thomas Fields.

Until we meet again! That is the meaning
Of the familiar words, that men repeat
At parting in the street.
Ah yes, till then! But when death intervening
Rends us asunder, with what ceaseless pain
We wait for the Again!

The friends who leave us do not feel the sorrow
Of parting, as we feel it, who must stay
Lamenting day by day,
And knowing, when we wake upon the morrow,
We shall not find it its accustomed place
The one beloved face.

It were a double grief, if the departed,
Being released from earth, should still retain
A sense of earthly pain;
It were a double grief, if the true-hearted,
Who loved us here, should on the further shore
Remember us no more.

Believing, in the midst of our afflictions,
That death is a beginning, not an end,
We cry to them, and send
Farewells, that better might be called predictions,
Being fore-shadowings of the future, thrown
Into the vast Unknown.

Faith overleaps the confines of our reason
And if by faith, as in old times was said,
Women received their dead
Raised up to life, then only for a season
Our partings are, nor shall we wait in vain
Until we meet again!

TRIBUTES

After Fanny Longfellow's death, Longfellow found consolation in translating, with a group of friends, Dante's Divine Comedy. *He continued to write and translate poems until 1882 when he died, at the age of seventy-five, of peritonitis (although, according to biographer Charles Calhoun, the symptoms suggest stomach cancer).*

The world—young and old—mourned his death. American children, who had once sent him birthday cards, now sent their pennies to build a memorial to "the poet who had always loved them." The monumental statue overlooks Portland, Maine—Longfellow's native town—and the names of all the children who sent their coins are locked in a box within the base of the statue. Across America, flags flew at half-mast. In England, the first bust of a non-English poet was dedicated in Poet's Corner at Westminster Abbey in his memory.

"Never was poet so mourned," observed scholar Charles Eliot Norton, "for never was poet so loved."

He was buried with his beloved wives at Mt. Auburn Cemetery in Cambridge, Massachusetts. Following the burial, a funeral service at Harvard College's Chapel ended with these words by the Reverend C.C. Everett:

> "'He passed away!' I think we have not yet learned the meaning of those words. I think we do not yet quite feel them. We still half think we may sometimes meet him in his familiar haunts.
>
> Does not this protest of the heart contain a truth? His spirit, as we trust, has been called to higher service; yet he had given himself unto the world, he had breathed himself into his songs: in them he is with us still.
>
> Wherever they go, as they wander over the world, he will be with them, a minister of love; he will be by the side of youth, pointing to heights as yet unscaled, bidding him have faith and courage; he will be with the wanderer in

foreign lands, making the beauty that he sees more fair; he will be with the mariner on the seas; he will be in the quiet beauty of home; he will be by the side of the sorrowing heart, pointing to a higher faith. When old age is gathering about the human soul, he will be there still, to cry that 'age is opportunity no less than youth itself.'

Thus will he inspire faith and courage in all, and point us to those two sources of strength that never fail,—'Heart within, and God o'erhead.'"

Charles Eliot Norton adds:

"His spirit will continue to soften, to refine, and to elevate the hearts of men. He will be the beloved friend of future generations as he has been of his own. His desire will be gratified:

[*Norton finishes with the following lines from Longfellow's* The Golden Legend.]

'And in your life let my remembrance linger,
As something not to trouble and disturb it,
But to complete it, adding life to life.
And if at times beside the evening fire
You see my face among the other faces,
Let it not be regarded as a ghost
That haunts your home, but as a guest who loves you.'"

Notes

Voices of the Night benefits from letters, journals, and stories from multiple sources that can be found in the endnotes below. For easy review, each note is organized by *Voices of the Night* chapter; italicized phrases to identify the text supported by a reference source; and the author, title, and page number of the source that's referenced. Please see the Bibliography section for more information on each source cited below.

Frontispiece

I am deeply touched Samuel Longfellow, *Final Memorials,* 203.

Chapter 2:
How Do We Live With Grief When It Won't Go Away?

The real danger Lewis, *A Grief Observed,* 5.

Try to love the question Rilke, *Letters to a Young Poet,* 35.

Do not seek the answers Rilke, 35.

Chapter 3:
Living the Question

In thinking to make a lawyer of me Samuel Longfellow, *Life,* I, 52.

He published the books himself Thompson, *Young Longfellow,* 152.

You call it a dog's life Ibid., 168.

At the time, Portland was regionally famous Higginson, *Henry Wadsworth Longfellow*, 61. Thomas Wentworth Higginson was a nephew by marriage to Mary Potter. He married her niece and namesake, Mary Potter Thaxter.

something was still wanting Samuel Longfellow, *Life,* I, 191.

Among the ladies Ibid., 191.

He begged his sister Higginson, 60.

Her notebooks, preserved by her family Kennedy, *Henry W. Longfellow: Biography, Anecdote, Letters, Criticism,* 40.

According to Longfellow biographer Ibid., 40.

She was a lovely woman Higginson, 64.

I have never seen a woman Hilen, I, 348.

My first impression of her Higginson, 61.

They were tenderly devoted to each other Samuel Longfellow, *Life,* I, 188.

Clara Crowninshield, a friend of Mary's, joined them In addition to Clara, the party initially included Mary's cousin, Mary Goddard, who departed early due to the death of her father.

We are generally taken for French Higginson, 88.

Mr. and Mrs. Carlyle Ibid., 92.

My dear Aunt Lucia Ibid., 100.

If it cheers a lonely winter's evening Ibid., 98.

We are unfortunately on the north side of the house Crowninshield, *Diary: A European Tour with Longfellow, 1835-1836,* 160.

It won't do me any good Crowninshield, 177.

How often I recall you Mary Thatcher Higginson, *New Longfellow Letters,* Harper's Monthly Magazine, CVI, 786.

According to Mary's niece Ibid., 786.

he stumbled out of the room Crowninshield, 181.

My poor Mary is worse today Thompson, 223.

Are you breathing easier Crowninshield, 183.

In death as in life Hilen I, 528.

Dear, little Clara Crowninshield, 182.

How my poor father will mourn Higginson, 110.

My father has always been kind Crowninshield, 183. The final dialogue between Mary and Longfellow is drawn from both Longfellow's account found in Higginson's *Henry Wadsworth Longfellow* (107-111) and Crowninshield's account found in her *Diary* (181-183).

Why should I be troubled Higginson, 110.

I will be with you Samuel Longfellow, *Life,* I, 215.

who had become "as a sister" Hilen, I, 525.

Now that there was no longer cause for restraint Crowninshield, 215.

Peace! Peace! Higginson, 111.

If I get to Heidelburg Hilen, I, 550.

I feel lonely and dejected Samuel Longfellow, *Life,* I, 218.

When I think how gentle Ibid., 218.

Longfellow tried to write Wagenknecht, *Henry Wadsworth Longfellow,*161. Wagenecht found the letter from Longfellow to his mentor, George Ticknor, in the Dartmouth College Library collection.

But, oh! As to embrace me Milton, "On His Deceased Wife," *An Anthology of English Literature,* 267.

To Mary in heaven Wagenknecht, 161.

I take no part Hilen, I, 543.

I feel assured of her presence Thompson, 230.

I cannot study Wagenecht, 161.

I am completely crushed Hilen, I, 543.

While resting by a lake Samuel Longfellow, *Life,* I, 225.

And now the sun Longfellow, *Hyperion,* 263. Also recounted in Samuel Longfellow, *Life,* I, 225-226.

Live in the Present wisely Longfellow, *Hyperion,* 265.

Live in the Present Samuel Longfellow, *Life,* I, 303.

Travel is not always a cure Thompson, 234.

What a solitary lonely being Samuel Longfellow, *Life,* I, 229.

Never let one thought Hilen, I, 566.

The day was pleasant Samuel Longfellow, I, 239.

My dear Eliza Higgenson, 113.

When the hours of day are numbered Longfellow, "Footsteps of Angels," *The Complete Poetical Works,* 4.

March 26, 1839. A lovely morning Samuel Longfellow, *Life,* I, 316.

Look, then, into thine heart Longfellow, "Prelude: Voices of the Night," *The Complete Poetical Works,* 1.

to rally himself from depression Samuel Longfellow, Life, I, 290.

read it to his class Samuel Longfellow, *Life* I, 281.

Trust no future Longfellow, "A Psalm of Life," *The Complete Poetical Works,* 2.

Chapter 4:
Footsteps of Angels

So much of the academic literature Freud, "Mourning and Melancholia," *General Psychological Theory,* 164-79. Twentieth-Century grief theorists, such as John Bowlby and Eric Lindeman, reflect Freud's earlier thesis, and work toward disconnection with departed loved ones as a primary goal in grief. For new grief theories that provide alternatives to disconnection, please refer to: *Dying and Death: Clinical Interventions for Caregivers* by Theresa A. Rand; *Grief Counseling and Grief Therapy: A Handbook for the Mental Health Practitioner* by William J. Worden; and *Continuing Bonds: New Understandings of Grief* edited by Dennis Klass, Phyllis R. Silverman, and Steven L. Nickman. For clinical research about resilience and stories of connection, please refer to *The Other Side of Sadness* by George A. Bonnano.

Bereavement Scholar Phyllis Silverman Silverman, "Living with Grief, Rebuilding a World," *Innovations in End-of-Life Care*, 2001; 3(3), www.edc.org/lastacts.

In an ironic twist Freud, "*The Letters of Sigmund Freud,*" Letter 239.

Mary's affection remained unchanged Higginson, 111.

Death is not a truncation Lewis, 58.

Strive not to understand St. Augustine of Hippo, "A Sermon to Catechumens on the Creed," *Nicene and Post-Nicene Fathers*, New Advent Online, www.Newadvent.org.

There are so many things to re-call Samuel Longfellow, Life, I, 407.

Chapter 5:
Connection to the Beloved

And as she pressed Longfellow, "Evangeline," *The Complete Poetical Works,* 120-121.

Words spoken by Longfellow's young wife Higginson, 109.

Shall I thank God? Longfellow, *Hyperion,* 243.

Do not forget me Higginson, 110.

the one beloved face Longfellow, "Aufwiedersehen," *The Complete Poetical Works,* 405.

This alone is health Longfellow, *Hyperion,* 265.

Chapter 6:
Connection to the Love in the World

Made the great friendships of his life Fields, *Authors and Friends,* 21.

Talk of matters which lie near one's soul Samuel Longfellow, *Life,* I, 284.

Arrow and the Song Longfellow, *The Complete Poetical Works,* 90.

Chapter 7: Connection to the Divine-Within

at a time when I was rallying Samuel Longfellow, *Life*, I, 290.

His poem inspired his readers Samuel Longfellow, *Life*, I, 271-272.

Frankl references Longfellow's poem Frankl, *A Man's Search for Meaning*, 131.

Mental Health Frankl, 110.

Messerschmidt grew up Bouchard, "A Majestic Voice," *The Portland Press Herald*, 20 Nov. 2004, C1. Cantor Kurt Messerschmidt's courageous story can also be found in "A Survivor's Story: Excerpts from the Testimony of Cantor Kurt Messerschmidt." The interview originally appeared in the May 2010 issue of *The Voice*, a Publication of the Jewish Community Alliance of Southern Maine, and can be found online at the Taos Jewish Center's website at: http://www.taosjewishcenter.org/hakol/hakol_summer_10.pdf

Noble Souls Longfellow, "The Sifting of Peter," *The Complete Poetical Works*, 399.

The Children were afraid Elizabeth Kubler-Ross, "On Death and Dying" (Lecture, Temple University, Philadelphia, PA, circa 1987). For another account of Kubler-Ross's use of the butterfly image, please refer to *The Cocoon and the Butterfly*.

Chapter 8: Grief Work, and Connection, and the Power of Consolation.

There is no grief Longfellow, *Hyperion*, 69.

The time comes for all of us Samuel Longfellow, *Life*, I, 302.

Effects require causes Drummond, *Drummond's Addresses*, 96.

our little schoolmasters Samuel Longfellow, *Life*, I, 301.

What may the morrow be Samuel Longfellow, *Life, I*, 319.

Act! Act in the Living Present Longfellow, "A Psalm of Life," *The Complete Poetical Works*, 2.

exquisite to read good novels Samuel Longfellow, *Life, I,* 324.

brain pan Samuel Longfellow, *Life,* I, 315.

Chapter 9: The Fullness of Melancholy

The swelling heart heaves Longfellow, "Resignation," *The Complete Poetical Works,* 129.

I loathe the slightest effort Lewis, *A Grief Observed,* 3.

What am I to do? Ibid., 10.

Will it be for always? Ibid., 66.

I sometimes think Fields, 21.

In the life of every man Longfellow, *Hyperion,* 264.

Two locks of hair Samuel Longfellow, *Life*, I, 377.

There was a mother The parable of the Buddha and the mustard seed is one of the most famous stories in the Buddhist tradition, and readers can find multiple versions of the story online. One engaging version can be found in *Stories of the Spirit, Stories of the Heart,* edited by Christina Feldman and Jack Kornfield.

One of his friends Maude Howe Elliott, *Uncle Sam Ward and his Circle*, 290.

Such ploughshares do not go over us for naught Samuel Longfellow, *Final Memories,* 399.

Chapter 10: Consolation Surrounds Us

God is in the space Buber, *I and Thou,* 182.

A secret climate John O'Donohue, *Beauty*, 233.

You think the dead we loved J. K. Rowling, *Harry Potter and the Prisoner of Azkaban,* 537.

It had been given to Mary Samuel Longfellow, *Life,* I, 302

Ah! Those melancholy anniversaries! Samuel Longfellow, *Final Memories,* 163.

Chapter 11:
Obstacles

Ah! It is not the sea Longfellow, "The Building of the Ship," *The Complete Poetical Works,*125.

better soul that slumbers Longfellow, "Footsteps of Angels," *The Complete Poetical Works,* 4.

I am to be married again Higginson, 172.

blessed memories to which I fervently pray Higginson, 174-75.

Chapter 13:
The Greatest Fear

All fear is rooted in fear of death O'Donohue, 215.

"Life after death" Please refer to Raymond Moody's *Life After Life* for a complete discussion of his research.

New research disputed the conclusion Neurological explanations for "out of body" experiences and "moving to the light" can be found in Sherwin Nuland's *How We Die.*

According to Hindu belief For background on Hindu tradition and the sacred belief of "OM," please refer to the translation of *The Bhagavad Gita* by Sir Edwin Arnold.

Strange as it may sound O'Donohue, 208.

Chapter 14:
The Wisdom of Grief

What is essential Antoine de Saint-Exupery, *The Little Prince,* 70.

The play "Steel Magnolias" Robert Harling, *Steel Magnolias.*

Talk not of wasted affection Longfellow, Evangeline," *The Complete Poetical Works,* 108.

Responding from London Jonathan Sacks, "Why does God allow terrible things to happen to His people?" *Times Online,* January 1, 2005.

We carry within us O'Donohue, 225.

Afterword

Out of the shadows of night Longfellow, "The Bells of San Blas," *The Complete Poetical Works,* 411.

Appendix: Nineteenth-Century Guidelines

I have not yet thanked you Elliott, *Uncle Sam Ward and his Circle,* 258.

poet-artist Washington Allston Samuel Longfellow, *Life,* I, 340.

Nathaniel Hawthorne Samuel Longfellow, *Life,* I, 337.

The benediction that follows prayer Longfellow, "The Day is Done," *The Complete Poetical Works,* 87.

Psalm of Life

I kept it sometime in manuscript Samuel Longfellow, *Life,* I, 290.

high resolve and wakened them Samuel Longfellow, *Life,* I, 272.

I can only send my greetings Samuel Longfellow, "Longfellow and the Children," *Longfellow Remembrance Book,* 76.

The Light of Stars

The poem was written Longfellow, *The Poetical Works of Henry Wadsworth Longfellow,* I, Riverside Press, 23.

Hymn to the Night

The setting of a great hope Longfellow, *Hyperion,* 8.

The Rainy Day

A dismal, rainy day Samuel Longfellow, *Life,* I, 251.

Mezzo Cammin

In 1842, he again visited Europe Fields, *Authors and Friends,* 21.

The Bridge

Life was too lonely Hilen, II, 536.

Resignation

Longfellow's journal entries Samuel Longfellow, *Life,* II, 118-123.

I feel very sad today Samuel Longfellow, *Life,* II, 128.

The Cross of Snow

The poet experienced more personal tragedy Samuel Longfellow, *Life,* II, 421-22.

Three Friends of Mine

My small tribute Hilen, V, 793.

Auf Wiedersehen

A sorrowful and distracted week Samuel Longfellow, *Final Memorials,* 300.

Tributes

according to biographer Calhoun, *Longfellow: A Rediscovered Life,* 249.

sent their pennies The majestic statue of Longfellow stands in his native town of Portland, Maine. According to historian Herb Adams, the names of the contributing children are in a locked copper box in the base of the statue.

The poet who always loved them Samuel Longfellow, "Longfellow and the Children," *Longfellow Remembrance Book,* 76.

Never was poet so mourned Samuel Longfellow, *Final Memorials,* 370.

He passed away Samuel Longfellow, *Final Memorials,* 358.

His spirit will continue to soften Samuel Longfellow, *Final Memorials,* 370.

And in your life let my remembrance Longfellow, "The Golden Legend," *The Complete Poetical Works,* 568.

Although contributions are not specifically noted in the text, credit must also be given to the Maine Historical Society which manages the Wadsworth-Longfellow House. Without the educational programs, preservation efforts, and opportunities provided by the Maine Historical Society and the expert MHS staff, I would not have experienced the far-reaching impact of Longfellow's life and work.

For further information about the Maine Historical Society, go to: http://www.mainehistory.org/

For more information about the Wadsworth-Longfellow House, and the Wadsworth-Longfellow family, please visit http://www.hwlongfellow.org

Bibliography

Arnold, Edwin Sir, trans. *The Bhagavad Gita.* About.com: Hinduism.

Saint Augustine of Hippo. "A Sermon to Catechumens on the Creed." *Nicene and Post-Nicene Fathers, Series One, Volume 3.* American edition, 1887. New Advent Online edition, 2004, www.newadvent.org.

Berman, Jeffrey. *Risky Writing.* Amherst: University of Massachusetts Press, 2001.

Bouchard, Kelley. "A Majestic Voice." *The Portland Press Herald.* 20 Nov. 2004: C1+. Print.

Bonnano, George A. *The Other Side of Sadness.* New York: Basic Books, 2009.

Bowlby, John. *Loss: Sadness and Depression.* New York: Basic Books, 1980.

Buber, Martin. *I and Thou.* New York: Charles Scribner's Sons, 1970.

Calhoun, Charles C. *Longfellow: A Rediscovered Life.* Boston: Beacon Press, 2004.

Crowninshield, Clara. *Diary: A European Tour with Longfellow, 1835-1836.* Andrew Hilen, ed. Seattle: University of Washington Press, 1956.

Drummond, Henry. "Effects Require Causes." *Drummond's Addresses.* Boston: George W. Setchell, circa 1900. 94-122.

Elliott, Maude Howe. *Uncle Sam and his Circle.* New York: The MacMillan Company, 1938.

Feldman, Christina and Jack Kornfield, ed. *Stories of the Spirit, Stories of the Heart.* New York: Harper San Francisco, 1991.

Frankl, Victor E. *Man's Search for Meaning.* 3rd ed. New York: Simon and Schuster, 1984.

Freud, Sigmund. *Letters of Sigmund Freud.* Ernest L. Freud, ed. 2nd ed. New York: Basic Books, 1975.

__________. "Mourning and Melancholia (1917)." *General Psychological Theory.* New York: Collier Books, 1963, 164-179.

Fields, Annie. *Authors and Friends.* Boston and New York: Houghton Mifflin Company, 1924.

Harling, Robert. *Steel Magnolias.* New York, NY: Dramatists Play Service, Inc., June, 1988

Higginson, Mary Thaxter. "New Longfellow Letters." *Harper's Monthly Magazine,* CVI 1904, 779-786.

Higginson, Thomas Wentworth. *Henry Wadsworth Longfellow.* Boston: Houghton and Mifflin, 1902.

Hilen, Andrew. *The Letters of Henry Wadsworth Longfellow.* 6 vols. Cambridge, MA: The Belknap Press of Harvard University Press, 1966-1982.

Kennedy, William Sloane. *Henry W. Longfellow: Biography, Anecdote, Letters, Criticism.* Boston: D. Lothrop Company, 1882.

Klass, Dennis, Phyllis Silverman, and Steven L. Nickman, ed. *Continuing Bonds: New Understandings of Grief.* Washington, DC: Taylor & Francis, 1996.

Kubler-Ross, Elizabeth. "On Death and Dying." Health Care Professional Symposium. Temple University, Philadelphia. Circa 1987. Lecture.

__________. The Cocoon and the Butterfly. Barrytown, NY: Station Hill Press, 1995.

Lewis, C.S. *A Grief Observed.* New York: 1983.

Lindeman, Eric. "Symptomatology and Management of Acute Grief." *American Journal of Psychiatry,* 151 (6): 155-160.

Longfellow, Henry Wadsworth. *Hyperion.* New York: Frank F. Lovell and Company, circa 1890.

__________. *The Complete Poetical Works of Henry Wadsworth Longfellow.* 2nd ed. Cambridge, MA: The Riverside Press, 1883.

__________. *The Poetical Works of Henry Wadsworth Longfellow.* Vol. I, Boston and New York: Houghton, Mifflin and Company, 1841, 1886.

Longfellow, Samuel. *Life of Henry Wadsworth Longfellow, with Extracts from his Journals and Correspondence.* 2 vols. Boston: Ticknor and Company, 1887.

__________, ed. *Final Memorials of Henry Wadsworth Longfellow.* Boston: Houghton and Mifflin, 1902.

__________. "Longfellow and the Children." *Longfellow Remembrance Book.* Boston: D Lothrop Company, 1888.

Messerschmidt, Kurt. "A Survivor's Story: Excerpts from the Testimony of Cantor Kurt Messerschmidt." *Hakol… TheVoice.* Summer, 2010, http://www.taosjewishcenter.org/hakol/hakol_summer_10.pdf

Milton, John. "On His Deceased Wife." *An Anthology of English Literature.* Roger Philip McCutcheon, and William Harvey Vann, eds. New York: Henry Holt and Company, 1931.

Moody, Jr., Raymond, A. *Life After Life.* 7th ed. New York: Bantam Books, 1975.

Nuland, Sherwin B. *How We Die: Reflections on Life's Final Chapter.* New York: Knopf, 1994.

O'Donohue, John. *Beauty: The Invisible Embrace."* New York: Harper and Collins, 2005.

Rando, Theresa A. *Dying and Death: Clinical Interventions for Caregivers.* Chicago: Research Press, 1984.

Rilke, Maria Rainer. *Letters to a Young Poet.* 2nd ed. New York: W.W. Norton & Company, 1934, 1954.

Rowling, J. K. *Harry Potter and the Prisoner of Azkaban.* New York: Scholastic, 1999.

Sacks, Jonathan. "Why does God allow terrible things to happen to His people?" *Times Online.* January 1, 2005, www.timesonline.co.uk.

Silverman, P.R. "Living with Grief, Re-building a World." *Innovations in End-of-Life Care*, 2001; 3 (3), www.edc.org/lastacts.

de Saint-Exupery, Antoine. *The Little Prince.* New York: Harcourt Brace, 1943, 1971.

Thompson, Lawrence. *Young Longfellow (1807-1843).* New York: The MacMillan Company, 1938.

Wagenknecht, Edward. *Henry Wadsworth Longfellow: Portrait of an American Humanist.* New York: Oxford University Press, 1966.

Worden, J. William. *Grief Counseling and Grief Therapy: A Handbook for the Mental Health Practitioner.* New York: Springer Publishing, 1982.

About the Author

GEMMA CANNON has provided both individual and group counselling to those living with illness and grief and has presented seminars on addiction, stress, and bereavement to Fortune 500 Companies throughout the United States. Her book, *Voices of the Night*, received the prestigious Nautilus Book Award for its literary contribution to the category of Death & Dying/Grief & Loss.

Gemma is a graduate of Holy Cross College and Columbia University School of Social Work. She lives with her family in Portland, Maine.